I0478417

HOUSEDOUBLE

The Smart And Simple Way To Start Investing In Real Estate

Tim Watro

COPYRIGHT

LIABILITY DISCLAIMER

Table of Contents

About Tim Watro

For the past twenty years Tim Watro has followed his *Move Out, Move Up* system to build wealth using real estate. He has bought, sold, and successfully rented and managed numerous single-family homes in California.

Tim's system is specifically designed for the average person to use and understand. He knows his system will work for the beginning real estate investor and create passive income for their future – because it's worked for *him*.

Introduction

Buying a House, renting it out, and repeating that process will be the smartest thing you can do for your financial future. The wealthiest people in the world use real estate to build their fortunes – people like Chip and Joanna Gaines of Fixer Upper have built wealth using real estate... and so can you! While you might not think so, you have something in common with these extraordinary people: You want to make your life better, you want to improve your finances, and you want to build lasting net worth! Congratulations – you have taken the first step toward reaching those goals.

The first step is the most important in any journey. You must take action.

My first step started when I met a man named Dave while playing golf. Dave was in his fifties and played golf a couple of times a week. As we talked I found out Dave was retired and no longer went to work each day. If you know anything about golf you know green fees are expensive, and I naturally wondered how he could afford such an expensive hobby.

What Dave said next turned on the light bulb in my head and set me on the path to financial security. Dave told me that over his working years he had accumulated five houses, renting them to other people... and he was able to live off the rent he collected.

WOW! That was it for me. I had to do what he did! I had to stop being dumb with money.

Even after the recent downturn in real estate values, I still believe real estate is the best investment you can make. Real estate investing has been a great vehicle for me, and I feel sure it can help you achieve your financial goals. This book is a road map to help you do what I DID, the way I DID it. Over years I have used what I call a "Move Out, Move Up" system to build real estate wealth. I will show the steps in my system, from buying your first home to getting the next one… and the next one… and the next one… building real wealth along the way. Like many things, the basis of the system is simple; the "devil" is in the details – all of which I'll show you. In simple terms, "Move Out, Move Up" is based on an easy to follow and fun premise: When you "move up" to a new home, you don't sell your current home – you keep it, rent it, and let others pay your mortgage (and expenses) on that property. The next time you move, you do the same thing. Each time you "move out," you add another home to your rental portfolio… and over time build real wealth. As renters pay your mortgages on your rental properties, your equity increases and so does your net worth – and at each step along the way you can "move up" to a nicer home. After some number of years you'll own a number of properties, debt-free… and the monthly cash flow you receive from rent payments goes straight into your bank account. Not only will you increase your net worth, you'll receive monthly income. In a way, "Move Out, Move Up" is an outstanding way to increase income and establish an amazing retirement plan – on your terms.

Sound great? It is!

Best of all I will show you the exact steps to follow. Theories don't help anyone. To succeed, you'll need concrete advice and guidance. You'll need advice based on real world experience. I'll show you what has worked for me... and can work for you.

So let's get started!

-- Tim Watro

Chapter One

Fear Will Kill All Your Dreams

I want to retire.

I want to have more time with my family.

I want more money I want a big house.

I want to....

Fill in the blank – what do you want?

Whatever it is you want, in most cases it lies behind a door marked FEAR.

Why do I say that? Think about it: Can you look back in your life and find the times when fear has stopped your dreams from coming true? I know I can' fear can stop more than financial dreams. Fear can stop any dreams.

So let's deal with fear. What is fear? Webster defines fear as "alarm and agitation caused by expectation or realization of danger." That sounds really bad... maybe we should quit right now!

Does that sound familiar, the little voice in your head that says doing nothing is easier? Doing nothing is always easier – while it eliminates your fear it also produces a guaranteed result: Failure. But hey problem solved! I realize that

sounds sarcastic, but that is exactly what most people do when they feel fear.

So what can we do to break through that door and get past the fear? Let's go back to the dictionary definition of fear. "Expectation of danger…" you mean like the time my family wanted me to go on this very tall and very fast roller coaster, man that thing was scary but they were able to drag me on that thing and off we went up and down and faster and faster until it was finally over? But once the ride was over it didn't seem so scary because I knew what to expect; if I went on it again I had the knowledge of what would happen… and as a result, my fears were gone.

If we gain knowledge we eliminate fear.

Simple!

So what are the fears in real estate investing, what does the little voice in your head have to say?

- *I don't have any money to invest*

- *I don't have good credit*

- *I have too much debt*

- *I don't know how to begin*

- *I am not good with money*

The little voice in your head has neatly packed your dreams in a little box and put them away where you can't find them anymore.

Do you really want to settle for that kind of life?

I don't. You don't either.

That's why there are a couple of concepts you must embrace before you can move forward.

First, is it possible for anyone to make money in real estate investing? Obviously the answer to this question is "yes." Some of the biggest fortunes have been built on real estate. That one was easy.

Now: Is it possible for *you* to make money investing in real estate? That question is tougher to answer, at least right now. Don't worry – by the end of the book, you'll know the answer.

Knowledge eliminates fear. Everyone is afraid of the unknown – I'll give you the knowledge necessary to eliminate your fears and free you up to start reaching your dreams. But always remember: Fear is natural – doing nothing is a choice you cannot make if you want to achieve your goals.

Chapter Two

Eliminate Limiting Beliefs

What is your thought process? Is your glass half full or half empty?

Have you ever said things like, "They were just lucky," or "I wish I would have thought of that"? That type of thinking can be put into a math equation that looks something like this:

No Goals + Fear + Excuses = Failure

I have a new math equation for you that can get you on your way to success:

Big Goals + Knowledge + Persistence = Success

Let's look at my formula a little more closely.

GOALS

Big goals... little goals... it doesn't matter the size of your goals. What is important is that to be successful you must have goals. In this case, say you want to be a real estate investor. That sounds like a great dream... but right now it's just a dream. Goals without action plans and without a timeframe are not goals, they're *dreams*.

This concept is very important: You must set timeframes for specific action to take place or you will not accomplish your goals. For example, let's set a goal right now.

I will buy my first house by this date_____.

If you currently have a house then you are already one step ahead on the path to wealth. You will have a different goal.

I will buy a better house for myself and rent the house I now live in by this date_____.

KNOWLEDGE

Once you have goals, you need the knowledge to accomplish those goals. In the coming chapters I will show you how I did it. I will help you avoid the mistakes I made along the way.

PERSISTENCE

NEVER GIVE UP, no matter what people tell you! NEVER GIVE UP! Don't let anyone hold you back or bring you down just keep going that is the difference between the winners and the losers. I love this quote.

"Winners never quit and quitters never win."

So which one are you? Are you a winner? No one is a winner every time, but the most successful people in the world have failed many times on their journey to wealth. The difference in successful people and less successful people is that the successful ones failed but never quit and never gave up. The game is only over if you quit. Successful people are persistent; they continue on and learn from their mistakes.

That challenge is now yours to take. Never quit and you can win. Quit... and the game is over.

Personal Analysis: Go From Point A to Point B

Life is a journey. Becoming a real estate investor is a journey. Becoming successful is a journey. No matter where you're starting from, that journey will take you from Point A to Point B. So let's take a look at where you're starting... that will help us determine how you'll make your own journey to real estate investing success.

So before we move on to the nuts and bolts of my system, let's take a look at your goals, your motivations, and your personal resources.

Why? Real estate investing takes time and effort. You'll need to do your homework. If you're investing in rental properties, you'll have to decide whether you've got the time and skills to tackle minor (or major) maintenance or repairs or whether you'll need to hire someone else to handle those tasks for you. You'll also need to evaluate your financial situation to determine what types of real estate investments are right for you both now and in the future.

Assess Your Personal Skills

If you like what you're doing, you'll be more successful at it. It's that simple. If you don't you won't... or you'll hate every minute of it even if you are successful.

Take a look at your own personality first. Do you enjoy working with people? If you don't becoming a landlord probably isn't right for you. (You can still invest in rental properties – you'll just need to factor in the cost of using a property management firm to deal with your tenants.)

Do you deal effectively with stress? If you don't taking on too much risk might not be the best move for you. You should probably avoid owning large commercial properties or buying foreclosure properties – at least at first. After you become more experienced you may find that taking on more risk isn't stressful at all because you have the capital and know-how to work through problems as they come up.

Take a look at the time you have available. If you're already extremely busy buying fixer-upper houses with the intent that you'll do the refurbishing work yourself probably doesn't make sense. The more work you do yourself the more money you can make... but not if you don't have time to actually do the work. If you're already extremely busy, buying rental properties and turning over the day to day management to a property management firm may be right for you.

If you're married, does your spouse support your real estate investment interests? Investing in real estate takes time – if your spouse isn't interested, you'll find it tough to devote the time you need to your investments. If you decide to manage rental properties yourself, you can expect late-night calls on occasion from tenants... and if your spouse isn't supportive, that can cause huge problems. A couple I know owns rental properties, and they have a "fourteen unit divorce rule" – they like to joke that if they own more than fourteen units, their marriage probably won't survive. Make sure you discuss your goals with your spouse before you get started.

Do you have any mechanical, electrical, or carpentry skills? If you don't, you'll have to pay someone to repair or refurbishing your properties. If you have the skills, keep in mind you'll have to have the time available to actually do the work.

Assess Your Financial Abilities

If you find it hard to balance your checkbook, investing in real estate will be harder for you. You'll need to understand the basics of personal and mortgage finance, and have a general understanding of taxes and other accounting issues. If you don't, you'll have to be willing to hire professionals to help you in those areas.

You can also take basic real estate classes at most community colleges. Some people even take the real estate agent preparatory class (a class that's required for prospective real estate agents) in order to gain knowledge about real estate investing. (After all, you don't have to become a real estate agent if you take the class.)

Work on Your Personal Credit

Your credit rating will seriously impact your ability to get financing, and to get financing on the best terms possible.

If you have poor credit, your options will be limited at first while you work to repair your credit. You can still qualify for owner financing, you can assume a mortgage, or you can qualify for financing targeted to individuals with poor credit.

Getting and maintaining an excellent credit rating is critical to investment success: you can get better terms and rates, and you can more easily leverage your properties. If you have poor credit you can still invest – people do it every day – but you'll have to be more creative (or accept less favorable terms).

Start Building Lending Relationships Now

Get a copy of your credit and make an appointment with a loan officer at your local bank. (Bring your own copy so the loan officer won't have to pull one, thus avoiding a new credit inquiry on your credit report.) Once you're there, show the loan officer your credit report, and discuss your interest in real estate investing.

The loan officer will review your credit report and can tell you what types of financing you qualify for. He or she can also give you advice about what you can do to qualify for better terms, bigger loans, etc. The easiest way to learn about what types of financing you can qualify for is to ask a person who evaluates potential loan candidates every day.

Now make an appointment with a local mortgage broker and do the same thing. You may get the same answers; you may not. Regardless, you'll be learning. In effect you'll get free advice and guidance. You'll walk away with a good sense of what you need to do to strengthen your financial position, improve your credit, and what types of properties and investments you can make through traditional financing means.

You'll also establish rapport (hopefully) with local loan professionals. That contact will give you a sense of whether you're comfortable dealing with that person, and can be a valuable contact later on... because you're a known quantity to them, not a stranger.

Analysis Chart

Now that you have a sense of your skills and financial situation, let's determine the best course of action for you. Real estate is an industry with so many aspects that anyone can find a profitable way to build wealth that is suited to his or her particular talents and interests.

Should you specialize in a particular area? You can, but you don't have to. Many people specialize in types of real estate that generate positive cash flow: Single-family houses, apartments, or rooming houses. Others find a particular niche and focus exclusively on that: rehabs and fixer-uppers, for instance. You can choose to start with one type of real estate, especially if you're operating with limited capital, and expand into other areas as you generate cash and equity.

If you're relatively new to real estate investing, you have to start somewhere. The following is a breakdown of how you can get started based on your financial situation, your skills, and your personal interests. Use this as a guide to determine the best ways to invest in real estate, and some of the best investment options, based on your individual skills, capabilities, and interests. My system is based on buying a home, living in it, then buying another home to live in while renting the previous home... and repeating the process. Each step along the way you add another home to your portfolio and continue to build wealth. But you can branch out into other types of investing as well, so we'll consider those options too.

- **Do You Own Your Own Home?**

Yes: Consider ways to increase the value of your property: Renovations, additions, improvements. Remember your home is an investment as well as a place to live – if the improvements you make are attractive to you, they will be to renters and buyers.

No: Unless you live with your parents (and plan to continue living with them), the first real estate investment you should make is to purchase your personal residence. If you're paying rent you're paying someone else's mortgage – plus you don't benefit from the appreciation of the property.

- **Do You Have a Down Payment and Good Credit?**

  Yes: Consider bank financing. You can probably qualify for excellent terms, and in addition you'll build a business relationship with a lender that will be beneficial in the long run.

  No: Consider seller financing or lease options. Sellers often are much more flexible in offering terms to buyers with poor credit. In addition, work hard to improve your credit rating – pay all your bills on time, and work to pay down your debts. The better your credit rating, the more readily you can get financing and the easier it will be to invest in real estate.

- **Do You Have Carpentry and Improvement Skills?**

  Yes: Consider rehabs and fixer-uppers. Instead of paying others to do the work, you can do so yourself – in effect you'll be paying yourself a wage in addition to increasing the value of the property. Keep in mind, though, that rehabs can take considerable time to renovate – make sure you have that time available.

  No: Focus on buying rental properties where less "sweat equity" is not required. Or, find skilled craftsmen who can do the work for you on rehabs or fixer-uppers.

- **Do You Like Working with People?**

  Yes: Consider buying and managing your own rental properties. You'll save on property management fees, and you'll build relationships with local lenders, government officials, and craftsmen. You may even rent to tenants who later will become buyers of other properties you invest in. In addition, you can consider selling your properties yourself instead of using the services of a real estate agent.

No: If you invest in rental properties, use the services of a property management firm. You'll probably also want to use real estate agents to sell your properties. Landlords have a number of interpersonal dealings with tenants; if you don't like working with people, managing your own properties will be frustrating.

- **Do You Have Solid Financial Management Skills?**

Yes: Consider handling your own accounting and bookkeeping. You'll have a better sense of the day to day state of your business. On the downside, if your investments are substantial you'll find you spend a lot of time handling the clerical tasks necessary to run your real estate "empire." At that point you may decide you're better off handing the clerical duties to someone else while you focus on finding and making great investments.

No: Educate yourself: attend seminars or take classes. Or, utilize the services of an accountant you trust.

- **Do You Want (or Need) a Steady Stream of Monthly Income?**

Yes: Consider income-generating rental properties. Properties with a positive cash flow (meaning your income exceeds your expenses) can provide you with extra income each month. Many investors specialize in investments in rental properties: they increase their monthly income, and over time build equity as they pay down the mortgages on those properties, and as the value of the properties increases.

No: Consider rehabs, fixer-uppers, options, and other shorter-term investments. Buying a house in poor condition, making improvements, and selling it for a profit will generate income, but not on a steady, predictable basis. If your goal is to build wealth instead of increasing cash flow, you can also invest in properties with longer-term appreciation potential.

- **Do You Have a Source of Capital to Invest?**

  Yes: Use your capital to make down payments, to purchase options, and to help you obtain necessary financing. You can also use your capital to finance improvements to your properties.

  No: Focus on investing in properties where limited capital is necessary. Look for little or no money-down loans, seek owner financing, and guard the capital you have closely. Don't sink all of your capital into one property unless you plan to sell the property quickly; otherwise you won't have capital available to make other investments until that property sells. If you buy rehabs or fixer-uppers, you may have to finance the repairs and renovations using outside financing like credit cards, personal loans, etc.

- **Is Your Current Income Level Low?**

  Yes: Invest in properties that yield a positive cash flow. If you don't yet own your own house, buy a home that is suitable for renting a room or portion of the home to third party. You'll lower your monthly expense requirements and can possibly buy a larger home than you could otherwise afford.

No: Invest in properties to build wealth or to make shorter-term profits. Of course, you can still invest in rental properties that generate a positive monthly cash flow, using that cash flow to fund additional investments. You can also rent a portion of your home to a third party if you want to increase your income.

- **Do You Like to Help Other People?**

  Yes: Consider buying pre-foreclosure properties. You can help people stop a foreclosure, find a home they can afford, and you can profit from the transaction. Or consider buying properties in less-desirable areas; you can provide affordable housing to low-income persons.

  No: Keep in mind that helping people can be profitable from a business point of view and also immensely gratifying on a personal level.

- **Do You Have a Real Estate License?**

  Yes: List your own properties and buy properties too. You'll save on commissions when you sell one of your properties, and you will be in a position to negotiate a better deal when you buy a property, since as the buying agent your portion of the commission essentially goes into your pocket.

  No: Consider getting a license for the reasons mentioned above. In most states you'll simply need to take a 3-month class and pass a licensing test. Once you've passed the test, you can place your license with a local real estate agency. You don't have to sell real estate full-time; many agencies will allow you to simply handle your own transactions. (Of course, you may also occasionally decide to list homes for friends or relatives, generating additional income for yourself.)

Set Goals

Most people spend a lot more time dreaming about success than they do planning for success. Dreaming is simply dreaming. Planning requires taking an active role in setting goals for your life and taking appropriate action to achieve those goals. Have you heard the saying, "The average person doesn't plan to fail; most failures occur as a result of a failure to plan"?

Put more simply: *Fail to plan... and you plan to fail.*

It's true. And setting goals is an important part of planning.

There are two basic ways to set goals. One way is to look at your current situation, decide what you can do, and then set a realistic goal based on the present. That's okay, but a better way to set a goal is to decide what you want to achieve and then work backwards to determine what steps you'll need to take to reach that goal.

For example, if you currently have a full-time job, you might say, "Hmm... I have an hour or so a night I can devote to real estate... so in six months I might be in a position to buy another house and turn my current home into a rental property."

Contrast that approach to the person who says, "Hmmm... I'd like to own five rental properties by the end of the year... what do I need to do to make that happen? I'll need to get my credit in order, start talking to lenders, dig through the MLS listings for potential deals, find a contractor who's willing to work with me if repairs are needed, and find an agent who might be able to help me locate good deals…. Okay, then my short-term goal is to get those things in place in two weeks. Then I'll be ready to start making offers on properties I think are good investments."

The difference is critical: The best way to set goals is to decide where you want to be in six months, a year, five years, ten years… and then develop action plans that allow you to reach those goals.

You'll have to make changes to your life in order to take those actions – but those changes will be worth it.

Short-Term Goals

Short term goals are things you can accomplish in less than twelve months. (You can create short-term goals with time frames as short as one day if you like.)

Examples of short-term goals are:

- Own your own home within four months.

- Own three residential rental properties within six months.

- Generate a monthly cash flow of $1,500 within six months.

Examples of extremely short-term goals are:

- Spend thirty minutes a day looking for suitable properties.

- Inspect five properties a week for possible purchase.

- Meet with two lenders this week.

- Contact ten sellers per week.

Long-Term Goals

Long-term goals are things you want to accomplish over the next one to thirty years.

For successful people, long-term goals are in reality long-range *plans*.

Your long-term goal could be to retire in twenty years due to the success of your real estate investments; if that is your goal, first you'll need to determine how much money you will need to have to live off, and then set intermediate goals that allow you to reach that level of wealth. Your long-term goal could be to own $10 million in real estate in twenty years, or to have a positive cash flow from your investments of $7,000 per month.

Here's a key element of the goal-setting process: Your goals are *your* goals, not someone else's. There is no right or wrong goal – the right goal is the goal that's right for *you*.

How to Set Goals

Goals are like building blocks: Extremely short-term goals support short-term goals, and short-term goals support mid-term and long-range goals. To determine your short-term goals, you'll have to determine your long-term goals first.

Let's say your goal is to own $10 million in real estate in twenty years. Great! Now you have to get there. You can break that goal down into manageable chunks:

- After five years: own $1 million in real estate.

- After ten years: own $3 million in real estate.

- After fifteen years: own $7 million in real estate.

- After twenty years: own $10 million in real estate.

Now you can break that down further:

- After one year: own two properties worth $175,000.

- After two years: own four properties worth $350,000.

- After three years: own six properties worth $550,000.

- Etc.

If you keep breaking your goals down into more manageable chunks, what seems like an insurmountable task – owning $10 million in real estate – can actually be quite manageable if you break it into small, achievable steps.

For instance, let's say you currently don't own your own home. In fact you own no real estate at all.

But, based on the above goal breakdown, your goal for your first year is to own two properties worth $300,000. How do you get there? Here's how you could break it down:

Goal: Own Two Properties Worth $300,000 in One Year

Week 1: Meet with at least two lenders to determine if I qualify for financing. If I don't, focus on seller-financed properties, see if relatives will co-sign on loans, and identify other creative financing possibilities by the end of the week.

Meet with and interview at least three real estate agents to find an agent I'm comfortable with and who has the kind of expertise I'm looking for.

Look at newspaper listings, internet listings, and local real estate agency advertisements for at least thirty minutes every day to get a sense of available properties and the local market.

Week 2: Choose an agent and make appointments to see at least four properties that fit my needs and financial situation.

Plan to generate as much capital for a down payment as I can: sell assets, shift money out of stocks or other investments (if necessary).

Call sellers offering owner financing, make appointments to inspect appropriate properties.

Week 3: Determine if any available properties are suitable for me; if so, assess their value and make an offer. Negotiate as necessary.

Find a good real estate attorney to handle my real estate affairs.

Week 4: Finalize contract (if negotiations are successful); if not, continue inspecting at least four properties per week. If successful, begin process of finalizing transaction; in the meantime, continue inspecting at least two properties per week for future investments.

...

Week 26: Make offer on second property.....

Etc.

If you work backwards from the creation of long-term goals to mid-term and short-term goals, you'll create an action plan that will allow you to reach your dreams. It's not hard to do, and it can be really fun – simply think big, and then work backwards to decide what you need to do to make your dreams happen.

To make your own goal worksheet, simply take a piece of paper and put your long-term goal at the top. Then, in outline form, break your goal down into intermediate steps you'll need to achieve. Under those steps, break down the tasks further. When you're done you should have short-term goals you wish to reach that are no longer than one week in duration – if you allow yourself too much time to achieve a short-term goal, you will be more likely to procrastinate.

Once a goal or task is complete, check it off your list. You'll enjoy the sense of accomplishment and you'll stay on track with your action plans.

Remember, you can revise your action plans at any time. If you find an investment that's too good to pass up, you might change your short-term goals. Just make sure you don't change your goals or your action plans due to a lack of activity or effort – you'll never reach your dreams if you don't take action on a consistent basis.

It will take work and effort, but you can do it. Thousands of people are successful real estate investors – there's no reason you can't be, too.

Making Your Goals Happen

Goal setting is fun – but you won't achieve your goals unless you take action. If you set big goals, that's great – but achieving those goals will take time. To achieve your goals, you'll have to manage your time properly. Many people say, "Okay, I set my goals… and it looks like I'll need to spend four to eight hours per week meeting those goals. I don't have that kind of time."

My answer to that statement is, "Yes, you do." You simply have to use your time more efficiently. Many of us are "busy," but how much of that "busy" time is truly productive? I'm guessing that a lot of it is… and a lot of it isn't. If you want to be a successful investor you have to manage your time well.

Here are ways you can increase your productivity without creating additional stress.

- **First, realize that "time" doesn't change.** No matter how organized you are, there are always only 24 hours in a day. All we can actually manage is ourselves and what we do with the time that we have.

- **Find out where you are wasting time**. Many of us waste time we could be using much more productively. Do you spend too much time on the Internet, checking email, or making personal calls? Track your daily activities so you can form an accurate picture of what you actually do. Remember, just because you are "at" work doesn't mean you're actually *working*.

- **Create time management goals.** Remember, the focus of time management is to actually *change* your behaviors. A good place to start is by eliminating the ways you know you waste time. For one week, for example, set a goal that you will not take personal phone calls while you are working. Or decide that you will- only check personal e-mail at night, after you're done for the day.

- **Follow a time management plan.** The objective is to change your behaviors over time to achieve a general goal you've set for yourself, like increasing your productivity or decreasing your stress. So you need to not only set your specific goals, but track them over time to see whether or not you're accomplishing them.

- **Use time management tools.** Whether it's a written schedule planner or a software program, the first step to physically managing your time is to know where it's going now and to plan how you're going to spend your time in the future. Just keep in mind you don't need a fancy system; a piece of paper is really all you need to stay on track of your to-do list.

- **Prioritize, prioritize, and prioritize some more.** End each day by planning the next day. List what you need to get done so when you start work the next day you can hit the ground running. Also be realistic: If you list 20 tasks for tomorrow, how many of them do you *really* need to accomplish?

- **Set time limits for tasks.** For instance, reading and answering email can consume your whole day if you let it. Instead, set a limit of thirty minutes a day, for example, for email — and stick to it.

- **Stay organized.** Are you wasting a lot of time looking for files on your computer? Take the time to organize a file management system. Is your filing system slowing you down? Redo it so it's organized to the point that you can quickly lay your hands on what you need.

- **Don't waste time waiting.** Whether it's a meeting or a doctor's appointment, it's impossible to avoid waiting for someone or something. But don't sit idle. Always take something to do with you, like listing sheets for houses you're interested in, an investment that needs to be analyzed, or just a blank pad of paper that you can use to plan your next real estate investment.

- **Do the worst things first.** If there are things on your to-do list you don't enjoy or wish you didn't have to do – do those things first. Every day you should list what you need to get done – and the first items on your list should be the things you least like to do, or are the hardest for you to do. Tackle them when your energy level is highest – you'll feel a sense of accomplishment and a sense of relief when they're complete, and you can move on to more enjoyable things.

I'm convinced that 90% of success is based on showing up – each and every day. Sure, luck, skill, and timing play a part, but *perseverance* is a major factor in success.

If you give up, you'll never succeed. If you quit, you'll never succeed. Every day if you keep moving forward, making plans, taking small steps, crossing items off your goal sheets,

and your action plans... then one day you'll look back and realize you've accomplished great things... and that you're capable of accomplishing a whole lot *more*.

Chapter Three

Cheap Or Frugal

I hear this all the time: "I don't have any money." It is true that many people have a hard time making ends meet. Virtually everything we buy has gone up in price, especially the necessities in life like food, clothing, gasoline, electricity. Many necessities seem to double overnight in price... so what do we do?

I hear the same thing from people making good incomes; I have friends and relatives and neighbors who say the same thing: "I don't have any money to spare for investing."

When I look at how people spend their money I see why they don't have any, they waste it on things that will not help them be financially better off. Advertising has convinced us that we have to have the latest greatest "whatever" to be happy and keep up with our neighbors.

You will never get ahead till you change your spending habits.

It is a great feeling to be able to buy just about anything you want – yet *not* buy it.

That's right, *not* buy it! *Knowing* you can buy something is often more satisfying than actually buying that "something." Why? You don't fall prey to wanting something you can't have... and along the way you have more money to invest in real estate if you change your spending habits now.

So let's put your financial house in order – you'll make your money go farther, work harder for you... and put yourself in a position to build real wealth.

We'll start with determining your net worth.

Calculate Your Net Worth

Your net worth, in simple terms, is the difference in what you own and what you owe. (Assets minus liabilities equal net worth.)

Determine Assets

We'll start with your assets. Assets are cash or items that can be turned into cash. Bank accounts, stock investments, etc. are assets.

Your home is an asset, as long as it has equity, meaning it is worth more – in terms of real market value – than what you owe. If you could sell your house for $200,000, and you only owe $150,000, your equity is $50,000. That equity is an asset. If your home is now worth less than you paid for it – which is the case for millions of Florida homeowners – your home is not an asset, it's a liability. If you owe $200,000 and your home is worth $180,000, you are upside-down and in effect your net worth is decreased by $20,000.

If your car is paid off and you could sell it for $8,000 it's an asset. If you just bought a car, and you put little or no money down, even though it's "worth" $25,000 it's not an asset because if you sold it today the proceeds wouldn't go into your pocket – they would instead go to paying off your loan. (If it sounds complicated don't worry – this process will help you figure it all out.)

Use the following Assets Worksheet to list all your assets. Remember, the actual value is what you can sell the item for, not what the item is theoretically "worth." A gold necklace that cost $500 isn't worth $500 unless someone will actually pay you that much for it.

Here is a list of some common assets you might have:

- Savings accounts, checking accounts, investment accounts

- 401(k) accounts, retirement accounts, life insurance policies (cash value, not the policy value)

- Home

- Automobiles, motorcycles, boats, RVs

- Jewelry

- Furniture

- Collectibles

- Antiques

- Cash

- Etc.

List your assets on this sheet:

Personal Assets Worksheet

Cash on hand   _____

Checking account   _____

Savings account   _____

Money Market Funds   _____

Home(s)   _____

Life insurance (cash value)   _____

Stocks   _____

Mutual funds   _____

IRA   _____

401(k)   _____

Retirement plan (current value)   _____

Automobile(s)   _____

Jewelry	_____
Antiques and collectibles	_____
Furniture	_____
Other	_____
Total Assets	$_____

List everything, but again, don't be tempted to overestimate the values. It's easy to place emotional value on an item that has little or no actual value. Your grandmother's bracelet may, to you, be priceless but is only worth $20 to someone else.

Think of it this way: If you die and all your possessions are sold, what would they be worth?

Also search for hidden or forgotten assets. You may have a savings account you've forgotten about, stock certificates collecting dust in a file drawer, savings bonds in a folder, or even old coins tucked in a cabinet.

Over the years it's easy to accumulate and then forget valuable items – hunt them down.

Determine Liabilities

Now that you've listed your assets it's time to list your liabilities.

Liabilities are what you owe. Any debt is a liability: Credit cards, personal loans, mortgages, auto loans, and even money you owe to friends or family.

Determining your liabilities is easier than determining your assets. In most cases you get a bill or a statement, unless a friend loaned you some money. (Regardless, that's still a liability.) Typical liabilities include:

- Mortgages

- Credit cards

- Automobile loans

- Medical bills

- Child support & alimony

- Household debts

- Personal loans

- Etc.

Use the following worksheet to list your liabilities.

Again, list everything. Take the time to think it through. This is probably a painful and depressing exercise, but don't be tempted to hide from reality. You must know your current situation so you can make good decisions and take the right steps to improve it – and possibly save your home.

Now fill out your sheet:

Personal Liabilities Worksheet

Mortgage   _____

Credit cards   _____

                            _____

                            _____

Automobile loans   _____

                            _____

Medical bills   _____

Personal loans   _____

Student loans   _____

Store loans   _____

                            _____

Alimony & child support   _____

Other   _____

                            _____

Total Liabilities $_____

Now that you've determined what you have and what you owe, simply subtract your liabilities from your assets to determine your net worth.

Total Assets _____ minus Total Liabilities _____ Equals Net Worth

For example, if you have $400,000 in assets and $380,000 in liabilities, your net worth is $20,000.

When you determine your net worth, don't be tempted to take shortcuts:

- Review all records and documents.

- Find actual account statements.

- Look up fair market values for your physical assets.

- In short, don't guess – know!

Determine Actual Expenses and Spending

No matter how much money we have, we all spend needlessly or without thought. To get control of your finances and determine your investing options, you absolutely must figure out what you spend.

A quick disclaimer: Determining actual expenses is at the top of most people's list of *least* favorite things to do... but is also why many people live beyond their means and make poor financial decisions. In your case the goal is to determine what you can and cannot do, realistically, in terms of starting to invest in real estate and building wealth.

How do you get started? First, gather up all your bills. Your bills will show your actual expenses for loans, utility payments, etc. (Your credit card statements will also show you how much you spend on certain items.) Pull out as many old credit card statements as you can – they'll help you identify money you've spent that you may not remember.

Then list all the ways you spend money – especially cash – that don't show up on a monthly bill.

Here's a worksheet to help you determine your monthly expenses. The list included isn't exhaustive – you're likely to have expenses not listed here. Write them in. Just make sure you list everything.

Note: No matter how hard you try, you may not remember all your weekly or monthly expenses. Take a week and track every penny you spend. Every time you write a check, use your credit card, or pay cash, write it down. You'll be surprised by how many ways you spend money that have become so automatic you don't even think about them... much less remember.

Expenses Worksheet

Mortgage   _____

Home equity loan   _____

Car payment   _____

Car payment   _____

Credit card payment   _____

Credit card payment   _____

Credit card payment   _____

Car insurance   _____

Gas and car repairs   _____

Home insurance   _____

Life insurance   _____

Child care and tuition   _____

Groceries   _____

Utility bills   _____

Phone bills   _____

Internet   _____

Cable bill   _____

Clothing   _____

Meals (eating out)   _____

Entertainment   _____

Other   _____

Other   _____

Total Expenses $_____

It can be mentally exhausting to put together your list of expenses, especially if your financial life has gotten depressing. Fight through it and identify everything you spend money on.

Then go back to your Expenses Worksheet and double-check to make sure you didn't miss anything. Have your spouse look it over. Find everything you spend money on: You absolutely need to know where you are today.

You'll notice your expenses fall into two broad categories: Fixed expenses and variable expenses. Fixed expenses are things you spend money on that you can't easily control or change. For instance, your mortgage payment is a fixed expense – you can't quickly reduce or eliminate that spending. Insurance is also a fixed expense; while you could shop for a cheaper rate, relatively speaking you can't decide today that you'll pay less for car insurance.

But you can decide to start bringing your lunch to work today, which will immediately reduce your spending. Groceries, entertainment, gas, clothing... all these are variable expenses, because you can easily make different decisions that can reduce your spending.

Take a second and look at your Expenses Worksheet. Which items are variable expenses and which are truly fixed expenses? For example, you may have entered $65 for your cable bill.

You probably see to that as a fixed expense, since it's a bill you pay every month, but in reality it's a variable expense: You could drop cable service altogether, or more realistically you could stop paying for premium channels you really don't watch. That's why cable is a variable expense – you can immediately decide to spend less. Almost every expense category on your sheet can, with a little creativity and a willingness to change your outlook on spending, be reduced – which puts more money in your pocket.

Before we move on, let's do a quick sense-check of your current financial position. Subtract all your current monthly expenses, fixed and variable, from your monthly net income.

(Net income) _____ minus (Expenses) _____equals_____ (your monthly surplus/shortfall)

What does this mean?

- If you spend less than you earn, that's great!

- If you spend more than you earn, you're in trouble and will have to take steps to deal with the problem.

If you're like most people, you fall into one of two categories:

- **Common monthly expense are reasonable or within your income, but you spend money on extras**

- Ongoing monthly expenses – much less the extras – are too much for your income level

Either way, I feel sure you spend more than you would like to... and if you want to build wealth, you first have to hang on to the wealth you have.

Determine What You Can Cut

Now you know how you're spending your money. I'm sure you've already identified ways to cut some of your expenses, but let's take a quick look at some of the possibilities you might have missed.

So: Go back to your Expenses Worksheet.

Take a look at each item on the worksheet. Pull out the bills or statements that document your spending in that category.

Then ask yourself the following questions for each item:

- **Do I need to spend this money at all?** For example, you may pay a monthly fee for cell phone damage or replacement insurance. (Typically that runs about $5 per month.) Does it make sense to have insurance if it will only cost $50 to replace the cell phone and the deductible is $25? Cutting off the insurance will pay for itself in three months. $5 per month may not sound like much... but it adds up to $60 per year that you in effect are currently giving away.

- **If I do need to spend it, can I reduce the amount I spend?** To use the cell phone example, say you pay $10 per month to send 200 text messages, plus an additional $10 because you always go over your limit. Can you convert to an unlimited plan for $12 per month? (Or better yet, can you decide the ability to text isn't really that important, and eliminate the charge altogether?) Take a look at every bill and consider calling to ask for a rate reduction. If you're not sure, just make the call and ask. What can it hurt? All they can say is no.

- **If I can't reduce the amount, is there another alternative?** Let's use cell phones again. Say your cell phone plan costs $40 and you get unlimited minutes, including long distance. You also have phone service in your house that costs $40 a month. Do you need both? Can you eliminate your home phone service and simply use your cell phone for all calls? (More and more people do.)

You'll be surprised by what you find if you're open to making changes. Here are few sources of savings you can find using this approach:

- **Cable, internet, and phone services:** Consider a package deal from your local cable or phone provider. You can get digital phone service, which is provided by a broadband Internet connection, high-speed Internet, and digital channels for much less than you will pay separately. And seriously – how many of your premium cable channels do you really watch?

- **Credit card rate reductions:** Call your credit card company and ask for a rate reduction. Simply say you want an interest rate reduction or you'll take your business elsewhere. If the first person you reach can't or won't help, ask to talk to a supervisor. If you have a $5,000 balance, even a 3% rate reduction in rate saves you $150 a year; even if it takes you an hour to get what you want, in effect you made $150 an hour for your efforts.

- **Auto insurance:** Evaluate your policy every year. If you haven't had an accident or a ticket, ask for a reduction. If you don't ask, you won't receive.

- **Auto loans:** Some finance companies now refinance auto loans. If you have a high interest rate and you can qualify for a lower rate because your credit rating has improved, you may be able to reduce your monthly payments by refinancing. But be careful; if you also extend the term of your loan, you may end up paying more in total. Check out the total cost, not just the difference in interest rate.

- **Meals:** Is eating lunch out really a reward for your hard work, or just a habit you've fallen into. Bring your lunch (better yet, bring leftovers), and if you need to "get away," go outside, go to the cafeteria, or simply take a walk. Even if you only spend $5 a day eating lunch out (and if that's all you spend, please tell me where I can get such a good deal), that's still over $1,200 a year. Still worth it?

- **Subscriptions:** Do you get a daily newspaper? (Better yet, do you still read it?) You can check out most papers online for free. Many magazines offer the same service.

These are just a few of the possibilities. My goal is to get your ideas and creativity flowing. If you're like most people, you've already thought of other ideas.

Well done!

But before we move on, one more thing: Watch carefully for the details.

Audit all your bills – every month, not just today – and look at all the fine print.

If you're like most people, you only focus on the bottom line, but the devil is in the details. Your hard earned money is in those details.

Especially check your credit card bills:

- Did you sign up for a credit watch program that charges you a fee every month?

- Are you still paying for a phone line you had disconnected months ago?

- Are you paying a yearly subscription to an online service you no longer use?

Inspect every credit card bill not only for errors but also for expenses you've forgotten. If a little sleuthing doesn't turn up some unintended spending, you're in a very small minority.

Reduce the Expenses You Identified

Identifying an opportunity is nice, but acting on that opportunity is what matters most. Let's make the process easy. In a moment you'll see a worksheet to help you work through almost all your expenses and find ways to reduce spending. Simply fill out the worksheet and then every day use the time you've scheduled to work on the next item on the list.

Here's an example. The following are monthly expenses. I'll use part of the Worksheet to help you understand what to do:

Reduce Spending Worksheet

Expense	Current Amount	Action Taken	New Amount Follow-up Required?
Cell Phone	$65		
Car Insurance	$50		
Lunch (work)	$160		

So far we've simply listed the current amount our theoretical investor – we'll call him Tom – spends on a few items.

Now we'll do a little work:

Expense	Current Amount	Action Taken	New Amount

Cell Phone	$	65	Changed	plan	$45
Car Insurance	$	50	Dropped towing		$45
Home Phone	$	40	Drop service		$0
Lunch (work)	$	160	Bring from home		$80

What happened? Tom called the cell phone provider and dropped replacement insurance and switched to unlimited texting between other people using the same carrier. (Everyone in his family uses the same carrier, so that works.)

He also dropped towing insurance for his car since in eight years she's never needed it. He also learned that her teenage son could qualify for a lower rate if he makes the honor roll, so he'll keep that in mind at report card time.

And he's started to take his lunch to work since he was throwing away leftovers, anyway. But he does assume he may have to buy a little more food at the grocery store, so he estimated he can cut that expense at least in half.

So: In about twenty minutes, he saved $20 on his cell phone bill, $5 on his car insurance bill (with more to come), $40 on his home phone, and $80 on lunch. So in effect he "made" $145 dollars – each and every month – for about 30 minutes worth of work.

Here's what you'll do. First fill in the first two columns of this Expense Worksheet. Then, each day, work on reducing the expense in one, two, five... however many items you can. Write down your savings – that will make you feel good about what you do. And if you start to lose motivation, remember that if you can save $20 per month after putting in an hour's time on the phone, for example, that's like making $240 an hour... because you'll save $240 per year for that one hour's work.

Reduce Spending Worksheet

Expense	Current Amount	Action Taken New Amount
Mortgage	_____	_____
	_____	
Car payment	_____	_____
	_____	
Car payment	_____	_____
	_____	
Credit card	_____	_____
	_____	
Credit card	_____	_____
	_____	

Credit card   _____   _____

_____

Car insurance _____   _____

_____

Gas   _____   _____

_____

Parking/tolls _____   _____

_____

Home insurance_____   _____

_____

Other loans   _____   _____

_____

Other loans   _____   _____

_____

Life insurance _____   _____

_____

Child care   _____   _____

_____

Groceries   _____   _____

_____

Utilities   _____   _____

_____

Utilities   _____   _____

                    _____

Utilities   _____   _____

                    _____

Phone   _____   _____

                    _____

Internet   _____   _____

                    _____

Cable   _____   _____

                    _____

Clothing   _____   _____

                    _____

Meals (out)   _____   _____

                    _____

Entertainment_____   _____

                    _____

Other   _____   _____

                    _____

Other   _____   _____

                    _____

Other   _____   _____

                    _____

Other   _____   _____

              _____

Other   _____   _____

              _____

Total Saved

              _____

One last note about this Worksheet: If you're not sure how to reduce an expense, it's easy. *Ask.*

Why? For example, most companies don't want to lose your business. Say you want to reduce the interest rate on your credit card. Call and ask for a rate reduction. Simply say you are looking at other options, feel your rate is too high, and you'll take your business elsewhere if necessary. If the first person you reach can't or won't help, ask to talk to a supervisor.

If you have a $5,000 balance, a 3% rate reduction in rate saves you $150 a year; even if it takes you an hour to get what you want, in effect you will have made $150 an hour for your efforts.

You can also ask for help. Call your electric company and ask if they have ways you can save money on your bill. Many will send you free information; some will even send an auditor to your home (often for free) to help you find ways to reduce your electric bill.

Many businesses will help if you ask; if they won't, and you have a choice, find another company who will.

Build a Budget

I know: The dreaded "B" word.

I'm sorry, but you need one – see a budget as your best friend.

Once you've worked through every item on the Reduce Spending Worksheet, your "New Amount" totals automatically create your monthly budget. Once you've eliminated what you don't need to spend and reduced what you spend on the items you do need, you know exactly what you will spend each month.

The beauty of this approach is you significantly reduced your spending while creating a budget you thoroughly understand. You know exactly where you *were*... and exactly where you are *today*.

Wealthy people became wealthy because they save money and invest it. They are not slaves to the lender; they make their money work for them... and they let their renters make them rich.

That's how you turn rags into rental riches!

Chapter Four

Finding The Right Mortgage

Unless you can pay cash you'll need a mortgage. Don't worry; almost no one pays cash for a house. To get a mortgage you'll need to find a good bank or mortgage broker.

First talk to friends or relatives and ask if they have someone they have used in the past they would recommend. The Internet is a great place to find all kinds of lenders you can check out. Once you find a potential lender, meet with them: Tell them what you want to accomplish, let them know that you want to build a long term relationship, and that plan to invest in real estate for years to come.

The first thing you need to do once you find the lender is get pre-approved, and find out how much house you can afford. Why?

If you've ever looked at a home with a real estate agent, you're familiar with this scenario:

You meet the agent at the property. As you're walking through the house the agent describes some of the features of the home. The agent also casually asks you questions about yourself: Where you work, how long you've worked there, where you currently live, if you're renting or own your own home...

Your agent is trying to get to know you. After all, they want to try to build a relationship, even if it's just a business relationship. But your agent is also trying to determine if you are a serious buyer and if you will be able to qualify for a loan for the home you're visiting — or for any home at all, for that matter. (If you've noticed, the same thing happens when you visit a car dealership.) Every agent is looking for serious, qualified buyers for the properties they show, and they'll work harder for serious buyers.

Now back to mortgage loan pre-approval. Pre-approval can take two forms:

- **Pre-qualified** means you have described your financial situation with a lender, and the lender is rendering an opinion about whether or not you will qualify for a loan. Pre-qualification is a lender's opinion based on information received; it does not mean the lender has reviewed your credit report, verified your information, etc.

  Simply put, a pre-qualification letter can be translated as: "I, the lender, feel this individual is probably qualified for a loan of this size if everything they told me about their financial situation is accurate. I have not tried to make sure the individual truly does qualify, however... so who knows how this will all turn out in the end."

- **Pre-approved** means you have provided documentation proving income, assets, and liabilities... everything the lender needs to evaluate your credit-worthiness. The lender has checked your credit report and most of the paperwork needed for your loan has been prepared. Sellers can be as certain as possible that a pre-approved buyer will be able to close on their home.

A pre-approval letter can be translated as: "I, the lender, have reviewed all necessary documentation and have run appropriate credit checks to ensure the individual will qualify for a loan of this size... I'll make the loan to them."

As you can see there's a big difference between **pre-qualified** and **pre-approved**. Real estate agents know the difference, and some home sellers know the difference. Getting a pre-approval letter provides several advantages that can save you time and money.

If you've been pre-approved:

- The seller can feel comfortable accepting your offer and taking their home off the market. In many cases a seller accepts an offer only to find out, sometimes weeks later, the buyer could not qualify for financing. They then have to put their home back on the market, losing valuable weeks of time and possibly having missed a qualified buyer.

- A seller reviewing several offers will look more favorably upon your offer because they are confident you will be able to obtain financing. If an owner needs to sell their home quickly, for instance, many times they will accept a lower-priced contract from a buyer they know can get financing.

- Completing the home purchase can be quicker. If you're pre-approved much of the loan application work has already been done, allowing your closing to possibly take place sooner. Motivated sellers may also further discount their home price if they know they can close quickly.

In short, shop for a loan and get pre-approved for financing *before* you start seriously looking at homes. At the very least get pre-approved before you decide to make an offer on a property.

Why do I recommend getting pre-approved *before* you start seriously looking at homes? There are several reasons:

- You'll know exactly how much house you can afford, which will keep you from getting stretched too far when you are shown that house that you "just have to have."

- You'll be in a better negotiating position when you do find the house you want.

- You won't be caught in the trap of hurriedly searching for a loan after you've found the house you want. Most home sales are contingent on you getting financing, and you're typically only allowed 30 days or so to get financing in place. It can be tough to shop around properly during that time – do it ahead of time and you can find the best financing deal possible. There's an easy rule of thumb: the bigger hurry you're in, the more you'll spend on your mortgage.

Keep in mind that getting pre-approved doesn't lock you into any one type of loan: It just lets sellers know that you can get financing if you make an offer on their house. You can still choose the right loan for you later on. For now, it's important that you know exactly what you can afford and can make an offer on a house with the confidence that comes from knowing you can get financing.

You'll be in a better position to negotiate with the seller, and you'll know exactly what price range of houses you should be looking at.

Types of Loans

Let's keep things simple. There are a number of different types of loans available. Stick to the basics: I believe that you should only get a fixed rate loan for 30 years... or 15 years if you can afford the higher monthly payment that comes with a 15-year loan. I believe this is the best way to protect yourself and keep your payments at a level you can afford.

The best way to keep yourself from buying too much house is to use this rule of thumb: Your house payment, including principal and interest and taxes and insurance, should not exceed 33 to 38% of your gross monthly income.

If you are buying your first house, remember, it will not be your dream home. Your plan is to eventually rent it to someone else as you move into a larger home... so don't over-extend yourself.

The key is to ensure your monthly payment is less than the rent you will eventually receive.

The Sub Prime housing mess, in my opinion, was caused by bad lenders and people who bought more than they could afford and thought that housing values would just keep rising!

Obviously they were wrong.

The good news is that this mess has created a great opportunity for first time buyers to get a house and start on the path to wealth and for current homeowners to move up and build a rental portfolio and financial security.

The only time I would consider taking out an interest-only loan is if I was buying a house with the intent of flipping it; an interest-only loan would keep the payments low while I fix up the property to sell it.

If this is your first mortgage, ask someone to help you work through the process. If you have questions, ask. Don't assume. To get you started, here is a quick rundown of the basic components of a home mortgage.

Interest Rate

An interest rate is the price of money, and a mortgage interest rate is the price of money loaned against the security of a specific property. The interest rate is used to calculate the interest payment the borrower owes the lender.

The rates you see quoted are annual rates. On most home mortgages, the interest payment is calculated monthly. So, the rate is divided by 12 before calculating the payment.

Take a 6% interest rate, for example, and assume a $100,000 loan. In decimals, 6% is .06, and when divided by 12 it is .005. Multiple .005 times $100,000 and you get $500 as the monthly interest payment.

Suppose the borrower pays $600 this month. Then $500 of the payment covers the interest and $100 is used to reduce the loan balance. One month later, when another payment is due, the balance is $99,900, and the interest is $499.50. The interest rate stays the same, but the interest payment portion is lower because the balance is lower.

The lower the interest rate you pay the better off you are. But you can't say that about interest payments, which depend not only on the rate but also on the loan amount and the term. Reduce the loan amount and/or shorten the term and interest payments will fall. Whether either is in your interest depends on the circumstances. Reduce the loan amount and you need to come up with more cash for the down payment. Shorten the term and you have to make a larger monthly payment.

Points

Points are fees the borrower pays the lender at the time the loan is closed. They're expressed as a percent of the loan. On a $200,000 loan, 3 points means a cash payment of $6,000. Points are part of the cost of credit to the borrower, and part of the investment return to the lender.

Borrowers typically don't have to pay points if they don't want to. While the rate quotes you'll see in the news media usually include points, virtually all lenders are willing to make no-point loans if you ask for them. (But, of course, the interest rate will be higher.) The rate/point quotes you see in the news are what the lenders view as their "base" terms. But they have other rate/point combinations they can pull out when they need to, especially if they're trying to land your business.

For example, a lender quoting 6.25% plus 2 points might also be offering 5.75% plus 4 points, and 6.5% plus 0 points.

The downside of points is that considering points adds one more level of complexity to a process that may already seem complicated enough. Most lenders can offer a wide variety of interest rate and points scenarios, but they typically don't show them to you unless you ask. Why? It's simple: Because most people don't ask – and that works out better for the lender. After all, they don't have to give what they're not asked to give.

Some borrowers have little or no leeway because they are "cash-short" or "income-short." If a borrower is cash-short they are required to avoid points in order to have enough cash to complete the deal. If they are income-short, they need to accept the lowest rate available so that the mortgage payment won't be viewed as excessive relative to their income.

If you have sufficient income and cash, your decision about points should be made based largely on how long you think you'll keep the loan. If you expect to have the mortgage a long time, paying points to reduce the rate makes sense because you're going to enjoy the lower rate for a long time. If you plan on selling or refinancing in the near future, avoid points and pay the higher rate because you won't be paying that rate for long.

Down Payment

In dollars, the down payment is the difference between the property price and loan amount. If the price is $250,000 and the loan is $200,000, the down payment is $50,000.

Many people confuse the down payment with the amount of cash they put into the transaction. In fact, the down payment amount is smaller because of settlement costs. For example, if you have $50,000 in cash and purchase a $250,000 house, your cash would be 20 percent of the price. But if closing costs add up to $8,000, you are left with only $42,000 to put down for the actual down payment.

A seller typically can't help a buyer with a down payment, but the seller can pay some or all of the settlement costs as long as that arrangement is disclosed to the lender. That is just as good as having the seller give you money towards the down payment, since cash that you would have used to pay settlement costs is now available for the down payment.

Here's an example: A seller offers his house to you for $200,000 and you're willing to pay that price. But under the best financing terms available to you, you need $12,000 in cash, and you don't have it.

So you and the seller agree that he'll raise the price of the house to $206,000 and he'll "gift" you $6,000. Assuming the appraiser goes along with it, the amount of cash required at closing drops from $12,000 to $6,000, making the purchase affordable (if you've got $6,000.) The seller gets his price and you get your house, so everyone is happy.

PMI

Lenders require mortgage insurance on any loan that exceeds 80% of property value. Private Mortgage Insurance, usually called PMI, is that insurance. The larger the loan is relative to the value of the home, the higher the insurance premium will be.

Again, if you don't know a lot about mortgages, have someone help you. And keep in mind any mortgage lender is required to provide you with a Good Faith Estimate statement that breaks down all the terms and costs of your loan. Make sure you understand everything on the statement – never sign any document you don't fully understand… and agree with.

Chapter Five

Finding A Good Realtor

There's a third party involved in most real estate transactions: The real estate agent. A good real estate agent can save you time, money, and effort. Can you invest in real estate without the services of an agent? Of course – but why should you?

A great real estate agent who looks out for your best interests is priceless. You can find one, but it takes homework on your part. Don't just blindly trust every agent that says the things you want to hear. Remember they don't make any money unless they sell a house, so their motives are not always in your best interests.

Let's take a closer look at the role of a real estate agent.

Real Estate Agents

There are two basic roles a real estate agent can play: As a seller's agent or as a buyer's agent. (And in some states a real estate agent can be what is called a dual agent.) By far the most common role an agent will play is that of a seller's agent. In short, they act on behalf of the seller of the home to sell the property. Because they work for the seller, they cannot disclose confidential information to buyers of the property.

Seller's Agents

In the past many buyers were unaware that the agent was not working on their behalf. After all, they may have seen a house they liked and called the agent... so shouldn't the agent be working for them? *No.* Some buyers would tell the agent the maximum they were willing to pay for the house, for instance... unaware that the agent could and would pass that information on to the seller. The agent represents the seller, not the buyer.

As a result, agents are now required to disclose that they are agents for the seller; in most cases the disclosure must be in writing.

While seller's agents are in fact working on behalf of the seller, they are still required to disclose "material" facts about the property. If for instance the roof is leaking, appliances are broken, or the heating system has failed, the agent is required to disclose those facts to potential buyers. Disclosure is also required if the property fails to meet zoning requirements or building codes.

Agents are not required to disclose personal information about the sellers themselves, though. The agent does not have to tell a buyer how motivated the sellers are, what their bottom-line price is, why they're selling the home, etc.

Buyer's Agents

Buyer's agents agree to work on the behalf of a buyer. They do not operate on behalf of the seller, so in effect the confidentiality relationship is reversed.

Most buyer's agents require their clients to sign an exclusivity contract stating the client will only work them for a specified amount of time. (In fact, some agreements state that you must pay the buyer's agent a commission even if you purchase a house using another agent.) Why do they require an agreement? They'll put a lot of work into finding a house for you and representing you – they want some amount of guarantee that work will pay off for them.

Buyer's agents can be very helpful. They also are required to disclose material facts about properties. They can research past sales to help you determine how much to offer for a property; they can help you negotiate with the sellers and the seller's agent, and they can help walk you through the closing process.

Why are there less buyer's agents than seller's agents? It's simple: If an agent lists a house for sale, as long as the house sells, they are paid a commission. It doesn't matter whether they found the buyer or not (although their commission is often higher if they do.) A buyer's agent has to hope that you find the right house and complete the purchase. Their odds of earning a commission are lower.

If you use a buyer's agent, you can negotiate the terms of your agreement. For instance, you can specify:

- **The geographic area.** If you're looking at properties in a fairly broad area, you can limit your agreement with the buyer's agent to a particular city or county, for instance.

- **The time period of the engagement.** You can agree to a long-term relationship (thirty, sixty, or ninety days), or to a time period as short as one day or even the showing of one house. Keep in mind that the longer the term, the longer you're required to work with the agent. On the other hand, in general the longer the term the harder the agent will work for you.

- **Basic exceptions to the agreement.** For example, you could negotiate that if you find a property that's being sold by its owner you have the right to purchase it without paying the buyer's agent a commission.

If you use a buyer's agent, make sure you understand all the terms of the agreement. The contract can state any terms you both agree to – so make sure you fully understand what you're agreeing to.

Dual Agents

A buyer's agent is a dual agent when showing a property listed by his or her real estate agency. Some states won't allow dual agency, because it's a little confusing to their clients: The agent has responsibilities to both parties. The agent can't disclose personal information to either client about the other, but still must make sure to meet the needs of both.

As a result the agent has to walk a pretty tight line.

It's easier to work with a dual agent if they aren't the person who actually listed the property. In that case they may not be aware of personal information about the sellers, so confidentiality is easier to maintain. If you have a buyer's agent agreement with a particular agent and he or she wants to show you a home they've listed, many firms will require the agent to "hand you off" to another agent in the firm for that showing and possible transaction.

Dual agency must be disclosed to both sellers and buyers in writing.

Agent Commissions

If you're selling a home using an agent, you'll pay a commission for their services.

If you buy a home, you pay no commission, even if you're using a buyer's agent: Their commission is paid by the seller.

Typically agent commissions range from 5% to 7%. That means if you sell your house for $100,000 and your agreement with your agent specifies a 6% commission you'll only net $94,000, because you paid a commission of $6,000.

Your agent does not pocket the entire amount of the commission, though. He or she only gets a portion. While some agreements vary, especially for newer or inexperienced agents, a typical commission agreement might work something like this:

Your agent listed the house. Let's say the commission rate you've agreed to is 6%. No matter who represents the buyer, your agent's company (agency) will get half of the commission, or 3%. The agent representing the buyers gets the other half. (If your agent or his agency manages to find the buyer for your house, the agent's company gets the entire 6%).

Your agent will then split his company's share of the commission with the owner of the company. For instance, if your agent works for Century 21, the agent will split the 3% commission with the owner of his local agency. ("Split" implies the 3% will be shared equally. That's not always the case. Some agents get slightly more than half; new agents typically get much less than half – sometimes as little as 30%)

For the sake of this exercise, pretend your house sold for $100,000 (I picked that price simply to make the math easier.) Let's look at three basic scenarios:

- The buyer was represented by an agent from another company; let's say she was from RE/MAX. RE/MAX gets half of the 6% commission, or $3,000. Your agent's company, Century 21, gets the other half. Your agent's agreement with Century 21 is that he will receive half of the agency's share, so he gets $1,500. The owner of his local agency keeps the other $1,500. So, even though the commission totaled $6,000, your agent received $1,500.

- The buyer was represented by an agent from your agent's company. It doesn't matter to your agent, though: he gets half of the 3% share of the commission; the other agent gets half of 3%, and the owner of the agency gets 3% (half from each side.) Agencies love when their listings are sold by agents in-house, because that maximizes their return. And in these cases, sometimes an agency will agree to lower an agreed-upon commission rate when the contract is being finalized... if that helps to sell the house.

- The buyer is represented by your agent – the person who listed the house. This is the dream scenario for both the agency and the agent. The agency still gets its 3%, and your agent keeps 3%. By selling your house himself, your agent doubled his commission. (That's why agents invariably show potential buyers their own listings first.)

Commission rates are by law negotiable. Let's say you're talking to an agent about listing your house, and she says her commission is 7%. You say you'd only like to pay 6%. No law compels her to stay at 7%, but her agency may have rules she's guided by. Some agents will automatically negotiate down to 6% or even 5% depending on how eager they are to list your house.

Well more than half of the time an agent will negotiate their fee downwards. Why? They want your listing. 5% of an actual sale is a lot better than 6% of *nothing*.

Some agents will say that accepting a lower commission rate will affect their ability to properly market your home. If they say that, find another agent. Others may try to convince you that if you'll accept, say, a 7% commission rate, they can do a lot more marketing and your home will have a better chance of selling.

Maybe some agents will actually spend more on marketing, but I doubt it. The average firm has marketing guidelines for their agents to follow, and besides, you should ask for a marketing plan as part of your requirements for an agent to list your house. Most agents will do similar things in terms of marketing; skilled agents are good at finding and working with qualified buyers, and more advertising isn't a guarantee of a greater likelihood of sale. (In fact, more houses sell due to multiple listing services, which agents use to find out about all the properties available in their area, than due to newspaper advertising.)

Agents will also sometimes say that if they accept a 5% commission rate that will keep other agents from showing your house, because if they find a buyer the commission rate isn't worth it. That's also not true. Again, an agent would rather have a reduced share of *something* than a full share of *nothing*.

Agents will also reduce commission rates as part of the negotiation to list your home. For instance, a few years ago I was buying a house and came within $1,500 of the seller's price. Their price was a bottom-line price, though, and they weren't going to go any lower. Their agent knew that, so she got together with my agent and they agreed to reduce the overall commission rate. The $1,500 came out of their commission: The buyer got the price he wanted, I paid the price I wanted… all because the agents took a lower commission rate. Many times agents will do this if it means salvaging a deal they may otherwise lose. Again, most agents realize a reduced share of something is better than a full share of nothing.

So feel free to negotiate commission rates. There's a saying many real estate professionals use: "List or die." Agents live by their listings: If the house sells, they get paid even if they didn't find the buyer. Most agents will negotiate the commission rate downwards even if it's only by.5%. And that.5% is worth it to you because if your house sells for $200,000, and you've negotiated a commission rate .5% lower, you'll have put $1,000 more in your pocket.

Once again, ask family or friends if they know someone they have used in the past and were happy with. A great agent wants repeat business from you, your family, and your friends. Interview several agents from different brokers, let them know that you will be investing in real estate and tell them exactly how and what you want to do.

A good agent will protect your interests, they know if the deal goes bad or they put you in a deal that is bad for you they won't get any more business from you, and you will probably tell your friends not to use them when they need a house. I know we talked about the mortgage but I must warn you some real estate brokers also have mortgage lenders tied to their real estate brokerage and they will try to get the loan from you also. In my experience they will not provide the best deal you can get so be careful.

Can you find a house without a real estate agent? Absolutely! You can search the Internet and newspapers and find lots of houses for sale. I have found that a great place to get a variety of information on houses is ZILLOW.COM. This website is loaded with facts on just about any house you can pick, just type in the address and you will get a price estimate for the value of that house, you can see the recent sales in that neighborhood, the size of the house, how many bedrooms and bathrooms, etc. Once you find an area you like you can check prices and other important facts before you meet with your real estate agent.

When you go to buy a car, don't you do your homework on how much the car costs so that the salesman won't be able to take advantage of you? The same rules apply in real estate; the more knowledge you have the greater your confidence and the less you have to fear. With that knowledge… and a great real estate agent to represent your interests… you can't lose.

Chapter Six

Go Out And Find That House

Now that we have gotten past the fear of investing, found a lender and found a real estate, it's time to take action and buy your first house…. or buy your "move up" house!

Here's my story:

I was 20 years old, living in an apartment in Brea California, a nice suburb of Orange County (or the OC as you may know it.) I was working part time in a supermarket. I had just bought a brand-new Camaro Z28; I loved that car. It was black and it was *fast*.

But the problem was I was spending all the money I made, because that is what 20 year old guys do. (I have been told 20 year old girls spend all their money too.) I was having fun but deep down I knew I wanted to be like Dave, my golfing buddy, and live off the rent of my houses.

I knew that was what I really wanted to do, but I also had to get over the fear. Every Sunday I would look in the real estate section of the paper to try to find a house I could afford – but remember, I lived in the OC and there was no way I could afford a house in Orange County. But I keep looking and never gave up… and one Sunday saw an ad for new homes in the city of Fontana for $50,000 dollars.

My first reaction was excitement.

My second reaction was, "Where the heck is Fontana?"

The next day I drove 60 miles east to Fontana to find these houses. What did I find? How should I put this... at the time, Fontana would not be anyone's first choice as a place to live. Fontana was home to the now-extinct Kaiser Steel. It was a steel town, mostly rural, but some new housing was starting to spring up. The words "master planned community" did not exist in the city's vocabulary. It was not the OC! But where else could I buy a brand new house with four bedrooms and two baths and central air conditioning for $50,000?

I went back to the OC and thought about it for a couple of days. Remember, I had a passion to buy a house, and my passion overcame my fear and I decided to buy the house. I went back to Fontana, picked out a house, and wrote a check for $500 dollars to start the process.

I was new to buying homes, and this being a new house the builder had a lender they had people use... so I let them do everything. I had no idea what was going to happen because I had never made such a big purchase.

By the way I did not have the $500 dollars for the deposit. I had to borrow it from Mom!

About 3 weeks after I met with the lender I got the phone call that I was approved for a loan... and this was really going to happen. It seemed like three years till I got that phone call but that call changed the direction of my financial life.

That's not the end of the story, of course. I had a very difficult time paying for that house each month, the payment was $120 dollars more than my apartment rent and now I had to pay more for gasoline because I had to drive 120 miles a day round trip to work.

First I had to decide what was more important: My car, which I loved but was just a car that would go down in value till it was worthless, or this house which would provide me a better financial future and grow in value over time. I sold the car and bought a more economical car with good gas mileage. I looked at all my expenses in the same way and made decisions that would allow me to keep the house. I did everything I had to do to keep that house. I ate hot dogs and chicken just to make ends meet.

I don't care what any of the experts say: That first little house made me what I am today from a financial standpoint. It was the foundation of my Move Up System. That experience started me on the path to passive income and financial security.

It is time for you to start on your path to wealth and freedom. Let's find that first or second house!

Location, Location, Location

You've probably heard that location is everything in real estate: If you buy well, you'll sell well. This truism is the cornerstone of real estate strategy, and here's why.

In less desirable locations, homes are cheaper and "good deals" are easier to find. These are often in areas of older and smaller homes, and buying one will cost you higher upkeep costs with lower appreciation. In other words, the years of mortgage payments and upkeep costs will yield less return on your investment when you sell.

Many first-time homebuyers assume that if they can find a home that needs minor fixing up, they can buy on the cheap and sell for a profit. Fixing up a home for profit *can* work if you do your homework and handle it wisely. Unfortunately, many people fall into the trap of adding on or remodeling a small home and over-improving for the neighborhood. In the end they create a white elephant which takes a long time and/or a big loss to sell.

Take a friend of mine; he made the mistake of over-improving his two-bedroom home when he got married and had a baby. He loved the neighborhood, had lived there several years, and didn't want to move. He and his wife decided to add an addition to the home to get the room they needed. Interest rates were down so they decided to refinance their mortgage to get the funds necessary. A local bank agreed to refinance their loan with enough extra to cover the $40,000 in construction costs.

The remodel almost doubled the size of the home and created enough room that my friend didn't have to worry about moving anytime soon. It seemed to be the perfect solution to his family's needs. But then two years later he got a job offer in another city that was too good to ignore. He needed to sell his home, but when he talked to several real estate agents he was shocked at the suggested sales prices. One agent explained why her price estimate was so low:

First, all the other homes on the street were two-bedroom cottages. There was nothing in the area as big as my friend's house. So the $40,000 remodel only increased the price by about $15,000.

Second, the lender had refinanced the home for about 120% of the appraisal value. (As you can guess, he got the loan before the mortgage crisis, when banks were making all sorts of unusual loans.)

Third, he didn't take into consideration the value of most homes in the neighborhood. In fact, he pretty much ignored them and ended up with a house that had a mortgage $20,000 more than what it would sell for.

Fourth, they assumed they would live there forever and didn't consider that employment and life changes can alter the best-made plans.

Fifth, a home mortgaged for 20% over market value will take about 12 years to pay down to break-even. Of course, the market can and will change several times in the next 12 years – but it's not something you can count on.

In the end, he ended up renting the house at a negative cash flow, paying $150 of the mortgage costs out of their own pocket, not to mention the cost of maintenance, upkeep, taxes, etc.

What to Look for in Terms of Location

The important key to remember is: The better the location, the more you can improve both the house and its value. If the overall real estate market heats up, better areas appreciate more. In less desirable areas, you won't be able to get back your investment on anything other than basic improvements, unless you buy at extremely cheap levels.

For example, there are older neighborhoods in nearly every city with small 900-square-foot homes built in the 1940s and 1950s. If they're near a university, downtown, or other desirable location, their value has probably soared. Yet, these same types of homes built near an airport or commercial center will sell for thousands less and will be much harder to sell.

In one instance, friends found a 1950s two-bedroom, brick cottage near a private college and close to an upscale shopping area. The house was purchased at an estate sale and hadn't been upgraded, but they got a good deal on it and were excited by its potential.

Looking at other homes in the neighborhood, my friends noticed that most had been remodeled or upgraded. Actually, their home was the least attractive on the street. It was a great opportunity and they took advantage of it by painting, restoring the woodwork, and upgrading the kitchen, furnace, and wiring. A few years later, when they outgrew their home, they had accumulated enough equity to put a sizable down payment on their next home.

So what did they do correctly?

First, they focused on the area. They looked for a neighborhood that would go up in value and was near a college, university, or popular shopping area, an area that would appeal to young professionals who didn't like a long commute, where homes had charm, and where similar people were moving in and renovating.

Second, they were careful about the money they put into the home. A large percentage of their upgrading required their own labor and cosmetic repairs. The money they *did* spend went where it would give them the best return: A new furnace and kitchen.

Third, they realized that eventually the house would be too small and they would have to move to a bigger home. Their plan was to accumulate as much equity as possible, and they kept their eye on what homes were selling for in the area.

Another big contributor to the desirability of an area is the school system. An area that has a reputation for good schools will have homebuyers actively seeking homes. Realtors will advertise that their listings fall within certain school boundaries, knowing they will attract serious homebuyers.

When you can find a good area with desirable schools, you've got a powerful combination for rapid home appreciation. In a seller's market, these homes will appreciate raster and hold their value better in a down market. You can go to web sites like www.schoolmatch.com and key in data for the schools in your area of interest to find out how they are rated. However, this is only one tool at your disposal.

You'll also need to talk to parents in the neighborhood to get a realistic picture. The bottom line is to go for the best location you can afford. A bigger house in a less desirable area is not as good a deal as a smaller home in a better area. In addition, always factor in the school system; it influences an area's desirability and value. Even if the dog and/or cat are all the family you'll ever have, it's still wise to buy in a good school district. Resale is easier and more profitable if the area has a reputation for good schools.

What to look for:

- Find areas close to colleges, upscale shopping, cultural, and sporting events. You'll notice that people are spending significant sums remodeling older homes.

- Find out what areas have the best schools and look for available homes within their boundaries.

- Look for areas that are close to where young professionals work and are moving into. When it's time for you to sell and move up, these are the buyers you want to attract.

- If prices in your interest area have steadily increased over the past few years, that's a good sign. Reasonably priced starter homes may be hard to find.

- New areas and subdivisions can be a good way to go. Values will tend to go up in the long term.

What to avoid:

- Avoid buying on busy streets and in high traffic areas.

- If the schools don't have a good reputation, this may be an indication the area is going downhill. If so, home values will follow.

- Before you buy, check out what type of people live in the area. If you find that the majority are lower income people, you may have a problem selling for top dollar or renting to someone else a few years down the road.

- If there are a lot of good deals and concessions, there's a reason. It's usually not too hard to find out the reasons why if you look around and talk to people in the area.

- If it's a new subdivision of starter homes and you plan on moving in about five years, others who bought at the same time may also want to move. This may put more homes up for sale than the market can handle, and prices can decline (or at least stay flat) in the short term.

Evaluating Properties

If you've done your homework and have identified the housing market where you want to invest, you're ready to start evaluating properties. Looking at houses is a lot like prospecting for gold, and I suggest doing some paperwork before the footwork.

Start with the real estate listing sheet provided by the real estate agent. There's a tremendous amount of property information on a real estate listing sheet, even though at first glance it reads like a laundry list. But the more listing sheets you read, the more you begin to dissect the information and get an idea of what to expect when you tour the property. Before visiting any one property, spend time reading between the lines of a listing sheet and use it as a starting point for questions and investigation.

Real estate agents use the Multiple Listing Service to electronically exchange listing information about properties. Years ago the information was kept on paper in binders or on note cards. While earlier information was cryptic and often contained limited descriptions, today agents (and you) can retrieve listing information instantly. This information contains the vital signs of a house — approximate square footage, architectural style, year it was built, sizes and numbers of rooms, type of heating and cooling system, type of siding, condition of windows and roof, school district where it is located, which, if any, appliances are included, and of course, the asking price and yearly taxes.

In the "Remarks" section of a listing sheet you'll find features the listing agent wants to highlight like, "Immaculate throughout this darling cottage." Depending on the writing skills of the listing agent, a listing sheet can exaggerate conditions with superlatives or provide no real details at all.

The listing sheet is your first exposure to a property, but it's basically a fact sheet used as a sales tool. You won't find negative information on the sheet, so it's up to you to inspect the property. Your first impression of a property is important, and your reaction will probably be similar to that of other prospective buyers. Make sure you don't overlook aspects of the property that can't be changed economically.

Here are some trouble spots to be aware of:

- **Standing Water on the Lot:** Standing water on the property can be a sign of poor drainage, which can be the cause of a wet basement or a settling or cracked foundation. Be sure to walk around the lot and note any damp, mossy areas and places where grass doesn't grow. Some drainage problems are easy to fix, but if the lot seems damp or you see standing water, make sure you investigate further.

- **Water and Moisture Damage:** Rain, snow, and moisture can cause damage to several parts of a house, such as wood rotting in the soffits where there's no ventilation, or moss growing on roof shingles or the siding on the north side of the house. These telltale signs are a tip-off to look for other indications of water damage throughout the house, such as in the attic for signs of rotten sheeting or rafters.

  Dampness can also promote the growth of mold and mildew, which mean more trouble. Water damage can be prevented with proper maintenance, but if neglected over time, the damage can be expensive to repair. Any signs of neglect should cause you to take a second look.

- **Structural Problems:** Major structural problems such as a cracked or settling foundation can be very expensive to fix. Unless you can get a firm estimate on the repair cost and use the amount to negotiate a lower purchase price, don't consider the property. Carefully explore the cause of large cracks in walls, especially in corners. Large horizontal cracks can be a tip-off to foundation movement.

- **Underground Tanks:** Underground tanks of any type can become an environmental disaster if they have been leaking for years. Be sure to check the location of heating oil, propane, or gasoline tanks on the property. You don't want to discover when excavating the foundation for an addition that you have a large oil spill in the backyard.

- **Well and Septic Systems:** If the property doesn't have public water and sewer, ask about the condition of its well and septic system. Septic field failure can produce wet areas and poor drainage.

Think about the Future

My Move Up System is based on developing a number of rental properties you will own. Every house you live in will eventually become a rental... so think about each purchase with renting in mind.

Fortunately, when you evaluate a house for its suitability as an eventual rental property you'll use the same principles you used to evaluate a home you want to live in: Location, condition, attractiveness, investment potential... and in addition you will also evaluate its potential cash flow.

Your goal is to purchase a property where the rental income will exceed your operating expenses. In some cases a negative cash flow can make sense, but if you're a beginner investor and you have little access to cash reserves, try to find a property you can rent for more than your expenses.

Also, because it's intended to be a rental property, don't look for new homes or for houses with lots of features like hot tubs, whirlpools, and other amenities. Why? Renters typically won't pay more for those features, and those features create more opportunities for to spend money on repairs and maintenance. The ideal house is a solid house in a well-maintained neighborhood. It doesn't need to be fancy: just clean, neat, and easy to maintain.

You can also find a property in poor repair to refurbish, live in, and rent later.

Here's an example of a good rental investment. A friend bought a small three-bedroom brick ranch in a small town in an older neighborhood for $210,000. The neighborhood was well-established and most of the owners kept their homes in good repair. The house was also in a good school district. The roof had been replaced a few years previous, and so had the heating system. She anticipated very little expense in terms of maintenance costs for at least the first few years.

Her "target" renter, or person she envisioned renting the house someday, was a small family eager to live in a house instead of an apartment – possibly a couple with one child, or a single parent with two children. Fortunately that target market is fairly wide – a large percentage of families don't have adequate credit or cash to purchase a home of their own.

Her anticipated expenses, including her mortgage, totaled approximately $1,275. After a survey of rental properties in the area, she determined he could easily rent the home for $1,600. That net operating income of $3,900 per year may not sound like a lot... but in her mind it was enough to take on the risk of buying the property.

She also saw further potential in the property. The house was located minutes from a local college where parking space was limited. The back of the lot had street access, and she could create a parking area for three cars, renting each space for $40 per month to college students. In addition, the property contained a small garage, again at the back of the lot, that she could rent as storage space to a local mechanic looking for a second income for $60 per month. Those two additions in revenue increased her net operating income by $1,200 per year, making her much more comfortable with the investment.

Here's the key: Some people buy more expensive houses with the intent to convert them to rental properties, but doing so carries more risk: The average person that can afford to *rent* a luxury home can probably afford to *buy* a luxury home. It is possible to make money by renting luxury homes to relocated executives while they are in the process of purchasing a home, but the chances of the property sitting vacant are much greater.

In short, if you buy homes where you would want to live... renters will want to live there too... and will pay you more for the privilege. And you'll build wealth more quickly – and with less risk.

Chapter Seven

If You Don't Ask You Won't Get

Once you find your first house you will need to make some decisions. My first house was new; I bought it from the builder. Yours may not – in fact, probably will not – be a new home.

No matter what type of house you buy, the key is to get the best price you can. The less you pay the lower your mortgage, the higher your cash flow... and the more equity and wealth you build. Many investors live by the saying: "You don't make profits when you sell... you make profits when you buy." Why? The less you pay, the more you make. You can't control what you sell a property for, but you can control what you pay – if the price is too high, you can walk away.

I will admit I knew nothing about buying a house the first time, but I have learned a lot since then and I want to help you avoid any mistakes and eliminate your fears.

Today you hear a lot about it being a "buyer's market" in real estate, and it certainly is. Housing has gone down in price in almost every area of the country. The best time to buy is when there is blood in the streets – and right now there's plenty of blood out there.

Where can you find opportunities?

New Homes

If you live in an area where there are builders have built a number of new homes that are completed and unsold, those builders need to sell quickly. Most offer big price reductions, upgrades, and even reduced interest rates and help with closing costs.

If you find one of these homes ask for as much as you can get. You won't get unless you ask... so be bold!

The more value you can get now the better off you will be in the future.

Bank Owned / REO

Banks don't want houses on their books. They want the principle and interest payments on mortgages on houses. Bank Owned or REO homes can be a good opportunity for great deals. Look in the real estate section of your newspaper or the Internet and drive around areas you would like to live in and that you can afford. Look for lawns that are brown and dying; these are signs of trouble and may be an opportunity for you to buy. Tell your real estate agent that you are interested in Bank Owned homes. They're out there – find them!

Auctions

Auctions aren't always the best place to find a home. If you bid on a house at auction be very careful. First visit the home if you can and get your real estate agent to determine what it might be worth, or go to Zillow.com and get an estimate. Auctions can be exciting and many people get caught up in the excitement and overbid for a house and overpay for the house. Beware of auctions; if you're new to real estate, my advice is to avoid them.

Then, once you find a house, do a little homework.

Inspections

When you buy a house your lender will order required inspections like appraisals and termite inspections.

In addition to any lender-required inspections, you'll want to conduct other inspections you specified in the contract, including a home inspection. Most contracts will allow you a specified amount of time to conduct the home inspection; if you fail to inspect the property within that time period, you can lose your right to do so.

Once the inspection is complete, there will likely be problems found by the inspector. (After all, it's their *job* to find problems.) If the problems are relatively minor, simply ask the homeowner to make the repairs to your satisfaction. Most will gladly spend a few hundred dollars to avoid losing the sale. If the problems are more extensive, you'll have to negotiate a settlement of the issue.

Remember that the homeowner was required to disclose problems he or she was aware of prior to the inspection. (That's why you ordered an inspection – you don't want to trust that the homeowner was aware of all the potential problems… because most aren't.)

Once problems are identified by an inspection, the result is the homeowner is now aware of the problem... and if you back out of the contract, the homeowner is required to disclose the newly-discovered problem to any future buyers.

In most cases, then, the seller will either have to discount the price or fix the problem to satisfy a new buyer. In most cases the seller will be motivated to reach an agreement with you. You'll have to evaluate the nature of the problem and the cost to remedy it as you decide what you're willing to agree to.

Other inspections may be necessary. Most lenders require a survey of the property. Typically surveys are considered "buyer" expenses, but that can be negotiated. In some cases if a survey has been done recently, the lender may waive the survey... but not all will. The lender will also typically require an appraisal so they can be sure the value of the property is suitable for the amount of the loan they are making.

No matter what, get the house inspected by a licensed home inspection company before you buy. The cost of this is small compared to buying a house with major problems. If you find problems that can be repaired and are not major deal breakers you can get the price of the home knocked down or negotiate other things to your benefit.

Everything is negotiable so ask or you won't get.

Negotiating: Emotions Are Your Enemy

Think about it this way: If you know what something is worth, it's easy to decide how much you will pay. Use Zillow.com to get estimates. Look at other similar homes in the area. Ask your real estate agent to show you comparables, or "comps," that have recently sold so you can get an idea of the market value of the property. Determine value first and then decide what you will pay.

And never, ever pay more than your price. *Never.* There are other deals out there. No deal is too good to pass up. No deal is the last deal you'll find.

In short, don't let your emotions put you in the wrong house. It is very easy to get caught up in the deal and lose sight of the objective at hand. Your first house – or your second or third house – is not going to be the dream home. You will use it as a rental once you move out and buy a better one to live in. Make sure it is a good candidate to rent out and that the numbers make sense.

The bottom line is to be a successful investor. Negotiate for the lowest price possible and make sure the numbers work.

That's the bottom line.

Chapter Eight

The Next Step- House Hack

If you already have a house you're ready for the next step. If you recently purchased your first house it's time to take the next step.

What's the next step?

Move out and move up!

Let's get going!

Step One

Here is the process in a nutshell: You will move out of your current home, rent it to someone else, and purchase and move into another home.

Simple.

But it does require action.

Your first step is to determine how much you can rent your house for. (Later I'll show you how to maximize the rent you can charge.) Start your search in your local newspaper: Find rentals in your city, call the numbers listed, and get all the information you can. Write down key facts like location, square footage, number of bedrooms and bathrooms, amenities like air conditioning or dishwashers, size of the yard, whether pets are allowed... get as much information as you can.

Then drive by and check out the property in person. The more you know the more you can charge.

Confused? That's okay; let's look at a few examples.

House 1: Three bedrooms two bath home with central air and heating, a dishwasher a two-car garage, nice backyard in a good neighborhood. 1450 square feet, and the rent is $1600 dollars a month.

House 2: Four bedrooms two and one half baths with central air and heat. The kitchen is nice and has a dishwasher. The backyard is also good and they provide a gardener. 1700 square feet, and the rent is $1750 dollars a month.

Now: Your house has four bedrooms and two baths, you have central air and heat, and the yard is well maintained. You have a two-car garage and a nice neighborhood and you will provide a gardener. In the examples above both houses are in good shape, just like yours, and they are in nice neighborhoods. You could probably rent your house for $1700 dollars a month.

What I have found is that if you offer a quality house you will be able to command a better rent than your competition, so experiment at first and ask for a higher rent; if you don't get a lot of interest in the property you can adjust the rent down a little.

Step Two

While you are waiting to close on your move up house, get your old house ready to rent. You know this house inside and out and you know what needs to be taken care of before your renters move in so get it done. If you are going to provide a gardener and you don't have one now find one before you rent the house. Providing a gardener is a nice perk for your tenants and it will help you command a higher rent.

Step Three

You will need some legal paperwork to rent your house out and protect your interests. Here is a list of what you will need.

The Rental Application: Prospective tenants will need this form to provide you with all their personal information.

Employment Verification: This form allows you to verify that the applicants work where they say they work and earn what they say they earn.

Credit Verification: This form gives you permission to run the prospective tenants credit report and see what kind of history of payment and credit score they have.

Rental Agreement: This is the legal document that defines the terms of the tenants living in your property.

Property Condition Checklist: I use this form when I do a walk thru with the new tenants when they get the keys to the property.

All of the forms above can be obtained at your local office supply stores like Staples and Office Depot and on the Internet. (And I've included some in the Appendix that you can use as examples.)

Increase Your Rental Income

If you own rental property you can probably increase the amount you make every month without spending much money. And if you do spend money making improvements rather than repairs, those expenses are deductible.

Keep this in mind: You're providing a *service*, not just housing – so look for ways to add services to your property.

Rent Parking: If you have extra spots, consider renting spaces to people who aren't tenants. (Or you can rent to tenants if they have more than a couple of cars.) You likely already have room for a certain number of cars per tenant. If a tenant needs more spaces, charge for it. If your unit is near an area with limited parking available, you may be able to rent spots to non-tenants. Some property owners located near colleges, stadiums, or other venues rent parking space for events or games.

Add Laundry Facilities: Study your competition first. If the average nearby rental property furnishes laundry facilities, you'll need your own in order to compete – or you'll need to charge a little less, not more, for your units. You may be able to furnish hookups and require tenants to have their own washer and dryer. If you tend to rent to younger people, you may create a competitive advantage by providing a washer and dryer. (Who likes going to the laundry mat?)

Create Storage Space: Most people need places to keep extra stuff; if you have the space, you can charge for solving that problem. Most tenants will appreciate (and pay more for) the chance to store items on the property instead of at a storage unit located somewhere else. Consider converting a garage or other building into storage spaces, or even building a new storage unit onsite. (You can even rent storage space to non-tenants if you like, just like you can with parking spots.)

Offer Additional Services: Depending on your market and where your units are located, renters may need – or be happy to pay for – other services. You could add a swing set or a small playground for families to enjoy. Think about what amenities or services your tenants might appreciate and that can help you charge a premium for your houses.

Add More Space You Can Rent: If you do it right, adding more rentable space to a unit could increase your property's value while you can also add to your rental income. Say the house has an attic or basement that's currently unused; if you can convert those spaces into a rentable apartment, your income will increase automatically.

The key is to make sure any new space you create should not detract from your other units. Keep in mind that you'll want the new space you create to match the style and theme of your other units. Don't throw up a few walls, install a sink and a shower, and advertise an attic as a "studio apartment." You may be able to charge more rent, but you also could negatively impact the overall appeal of the property – which could lower its actual value, too. Whenever you consider making a change, make sure it lets you charge more rent and increases the value of the property at the same time. (In most cases those changes should raise the property value, because increasing rental income typically increases the overall value of a rental property at the same time. And that's your goal!)

But, before you start working on creating more space, think about the type of people you're targeting.

If you're thinking about turning an unused attic into a studio apartment, think about your ideal renters and what they might need. If your ideal renters are students, they'll need room to study, so making sure there's room for a desk and possibly some shelves will help. If your ideal renter is someone just starting to live on their own, living space might be more important than storage space, since they're unlikely to be bringing a lot of "stuff" with them. (Think about your first apartment – were you concerned about cabinet space and storage space?)

If you're converting a basement into a small apartment, think about safety issues, and make sure the entry door is well lit.

And no matter what you do, comply with zoning and building codes. (If you don't know what your requirements are, find out.) Some localities require there be two possible means of egress (getting out). If you're converting a basement into an apartment and there is only one door and no windows, you may not meet building code requirements... and if something happens, you may be open to legal action. Try to add another door or suitable windows, and if that's not feasible, turn the basement into storage space or a common laundry area.

Change the Property's Use: Say you own a house that you're currently renting to a single tenant – that can be one person or it could be a family, but in either case you consider it a "single family residential" rental unit. With some work you might be able to convert the property to commercial use and greatly increase the amount of rent you charge. (Commercial properties tend to rent for much higher amounts than residential properties.)

- First check the zoning – the property will have to be zoned commercial already, or you'll need to get the zoning changed to that designation. You can determine current zoning designations and find out how to apply for zoning changes at your local government office. You may think a change won't be possible, but if you're converting residential to office, it's often not as hard as you think. In older towns, it's very common to see office properties on the same street with single-family homes.

- If zoning isn't a problem, then make sure there's a need for more office space in the area. Check local ads, and call a commercial realtor and ask about the current supply of office space – if there's a lot of space already available on the market, you may not want to change the use of your property unless you can fill a need that your local market can't meet.

- If you determine there's a need, consider how much parking you'll need. Your locality will have established parking regulations that require a certain number of spaces per occupant or based on the square footage of the building, so make sure you can meet those regulations. Also consider handicapped parking – in all likelihood you'll need at least one space, and possibly more.

- And last, run the numbers. Determine what it will cost to convert the property (construction costs, fees and permits, etc), and estimate what you think you'll be able to charge in rent once it's ready.   Be sure a conversion makes sense from a dollars and cents point of view.

Remember, your rental properties are investments – make sure those investments work hard for you.

Chapter Nine

Be A Good Landlord

Once you move out and move up you'll rent your old house – and you'll become a landlord.

And you'll be a good one.

What is a good landlord? A good landlord provides families with a clean and safe place to raise their children. A good landlord keeps the property in great shape and responds to his or her tenant's needs quickly. A good landlord has low turnover and fewer problems.

Best of all, a good landlord makes a profit and builds financial wealth over time.

That is what you will do…. and that is what you will be!

The first step is to rent the house as quickly as possible – that way your renters make your house payments for you. (Why pay the mortgage when someone else can pay it for you?)

While you can simply place classified ads, I go a step farther: I place an ad in the local newspaper and my church bulletin advertising the house is for rent, and I let people know I will have an Open House on Saturday and Sunday.

Why an Open House? I schedule an Open House – on my terms – so I can show the house to as many people as possible and generate a little competition between prospective tenants. I use a sign in sheet for people to fill in their names and phone numbers at the front door as they come to look at the property.

Keep in mind becoming a landlord involves a few legal issues. First, you cannot discriminate. You must give an application to anyone who asks for one regardless of what you think or what your impressions are – you absolutely must not discriminate against anyone. People will ask you how you decide who to rent to and my answer is: We use their financial ability to pay the rent based on their credit score and payment history – that's it. We don't discriminate based on race, religion, gender... it's a business relationship and a business transaction.

Here is something I do that can help you eliminate people who are not serious about renting your house. I ask them to pay for the credit check up front when they fill out an application. If they are serious and they have good credit they will have no problem with this request. This simple step will save you a lot of time checking out people who can't really qualify to rent your house in the first place.

Then I use a simple financial benchmark to qualify my tenants: The rent cannot be more than 30% of their gross monthly income. For example, if they make $5,000 dollars a month income their rent could not be more than $1,500 dollars a month. (In addition you'll look at their other debts, like car payments and credit cards, and whether they pay those obligations on time.)

The next step is to verify their employment by visiting their work place. Present the Employment Verification form to the employer; that way you can confirm what the prospective tenants have given you regarding their employment and earnings.

Next find a local credit reporting agency in your local yellow pages and get the credit report on the prospective tenant. You will need to bring the Credit Check authorization form they signed and you will also need a utility bill from the property to prove you are the owner of the property in question.

Now that you have the credit report and the employment verification you are ready to make your decision.

If everything looks good you are ready to rent to the tenant. Let the tenant know they have been approved, and schedule a meeting to sign the rental agreement. The tenant will need to give you a check for the security deposit at this time; let them know, in writing, that after 3 days even if they change their mind they will lose their deposit because you have taken the property off the market.

Next agree upon their move-in date. You will do a walk-through inspection on that date and collect the first months' rent; in return they receive the keys to the property.

As soon as you have the security deposit go to the bank and cash it to make sure they have the funds. Don't ever accept cash as payment for your deposit or the rent; ask for checks or money orders only.

The day your tenants move in you will do a walk-through inspection, using a checkout sheet that verifies all appliances, smoke detectors, plumbing, lights, and other items are in good working condition.

This is very important: The tenant signs this document stating the house was in good order and everything is working properly. That protects you from later claims that the property was not in good condition when the tenant moved in.

You will also go over a document I use which describes what constitutes wear and tear and what items are considered to be caused by damage. (For example, light carpet wear is expected and is normal wear and tear; rips and tears in the carpet are considered damage.) This is also very important because it clearly defines to the tenant the terms and use of the property and what they are responsible for when they move out and there is damage to the property.

The final document they will sign is the rental agreement, clearly defining all the terms of use and the timeframe or term of the rental agreement.

I like to rent month to month rather than lease the property for a specific length of time. That way if there is a problem it is easier to get the tenant out under a month to month plan.

Remember if you do your homework and put the right person in the house you will have a much better experience as a landlord.

Chapter Ten

A Lighter Touch- Use A Property Manager

Do you want to manage the rental house yourself or do you want to pay someone to do it for you?

If you don't want to get a phone call each time there is an issue at the house you will want to hire a property management company to handle things for you. The cost of these services is typically 8 to 10% of the monthly rent, and these services can include just about anything: Collecting rent, making repairs (within dollar amounts you establish), finding new tenants, etc.

If you decide to go the property management route, interview a few management firms and find out what services they offer and how much they charge and how long they have been in business. Also check with the Better Business Bureau for any complaints or issues with the company you are considering.

Keep in mind that even though they are managing your property *you* are still ultimately responsible for the property. If there are tenant problems, ultimately those problems are *your* problems. If tenants fall behind on rent, that problem is ultimately *your* problem. If tenants damage the property, that problem is *your* problem. The management company will simply help facilitate the remedies to those problems.

Property management companies will typically do the following:

- Screen tenants per your criteria, including performing reference checks, credit checks, and employment checks.

- Advertise and solicit tenants for vacant properties.

- Perform periodic property inspections.

- Coordinate repairs and maintenance tasks.

- Serve as the main point of contact for tenants.

- Collect rent payments, forwarding your portion to you (after they deduct for their fees).

- Maintain files and records.

- Coordinate eviction notices and eviction proceedings.

- Perform other duties as negotiated.

Keep in mind that agreements can and do vary – you'll need to thoroughly discuss the responsibilities and services the property management company will perform.

But You Can Do it Yourself – and Save

I manage my own properties and find that if you keep your house in good condition and do your homework in checking out your tenants that your problems are few and you save the money that you would pay the management company. To make it easier, I also have set up a list of repair companies that my tenant can call if a repair is needed such as plumbing or heating and air conditioning. I have given these companies a limit as to the dollar amount they can charge without my approval for the repair.

This has worked well and has saved me some late night phone calls.

For example, I owned one house I did not live close to and used a management company for ten years to handle the property. I got mixed results with this company: On one hand I did receive my rent over the ten years but this company did not really check on the property and inspect it on a regular basis. The result was that the property condition declined and was in bad shape when I had to evict a tenant. The house was a mess, and I learned a lot from the experience.   If you do hire a property management company, stay in touch and check on the property personally. Make sure the property managers do an inspection at least once a year.

I recommend that you manage your properties yourself as you begin to invest in rental real estate. You'll save money and you'll gain valuable experience. Later you can turn some or all the management functions over to someone else... but in the beginning, you can use the money you would have paid someone else to make more investments and to grow your investment portfolio.

But if you do decide to hire a property management firm, above all, clearly understand what they will do and won't do.

Chapter Eleven

Fixer Upper Exchange

Flip this, flip that, flip a house... I'm sure you have seen the television shows where people buy a house fix it up and sell it for a big profit. Flipping a house is certainly possible but is also not as easy as the shows lead you to believe.

Once you gain experience and have the right team of support behind you flipping is possible and you can make a good profit if you "buy right." I have done it successfully; here's what I did with one of my properties, using a process I call the "Inside Flip."

I had a house which I had rented for about ten years – the house I talked about in the last chapter, in fact – and during that time I used a property management company to take care of the property.

Wait: Maybe I should say that they really did *not* take care of my property and make regular inspections as to the condition of the house both inside and out. The house was not close to where I lived and I did not get to see it very often; I kept getting the rent on time and had very little expense so I was happy.

I was an absent landlord... which is not always the ideal situation, as I found out.

The tenants got divorced and had to be evicted from the house; this was the first time I had to do anything like that with one of my properties. Fortunately the management company handled it well and the tenants were removed from the house. But when I inspected the house what I found was a big mess: Every room was filled with trash and old clothes, the carpet was torn, the walls had writing on them….

The good news was that once the trash was removed it wasn't as bad as I first thought. Now my wife and I had to make a decision: Do we fix it up and rent it again, or do we sell it? Remember renters can make you rich, so I wanted to keep this house but I didn't like the direction the neighborhood was going so part of me wanted to sell.

Here is what we did. I only owed $85,000 dollars on the property and I knew the value was much higher. I wanted to take $100,000 dollars out of the property and use the money to pay off the house I was living in. Great idea, since you don't pay taxes on borrowed money and then my house would be paid for!

I had the house appraised. It needed to be worth $240,000 to make the loan work, and the appraisal came back at $240,000 on the nose.

Remember the house was a mess, so I was fortunate to get the amount I needed to make the deal work.

I could not rent the house in its present condition so I had to fix it up. First I got rid of all the trash and had the yard cleaned up. Next I had the inside of the house painted white and put down new carpet and tile floors to replace the vinyl. I put a new water heater and furnace in and replaced the dishwasher. When I was done the house looked great and I wondered how much it was worth now in top condition. I called my real estate agent to give me his opinion.

I was pleasantly surprised to find out I could list it for $290,000; just by doing some basic repairs it was now worth $50,000 more.

I now had to make another decision: Should we sell or not? The IRS has a provision called a 1031 exchange where you can sell your property and purchase another property of equal or greater value without paying taxes on the sale. So we listed the house for sale and looked for another house we could buy closer to where we lived that we could rent out. We only had the house listed for a week and received two offers at full price; and we took the best one and sold the house 45 days later. We found a nice house near us for $290,000 that was only six years old and in great shape; we bought that house and rent it to tenants.

After borrowing the $100,000 I owed $195,000 on the first house and sold it for $290,000. After paying the closing costs and real estate commission we had $65,000 dollars to put down on the house we bought which gave us a payment that would be covered by the rent we received. This was a great deal: We exchanged one rental for another, took money out of the deal to pay off our house, and ended up with a rental property closer to where we live that I could manage myself.

Win-win-win!

The Fixer Upper Guide to Repairs and Renovations

Some real estate investors build careers out of finding distressed properties and re-selling them after making repairs and enhancements. While my system is based on renting properties to others, sometimes it may make sense to sell a property for a profit instead of holding it to use as a rental property. So let's look at how you can maximize the price you receive – which maximizes your profits.

Let's start with the basics. Some rehabbers I know say, "Paint the walls, replace the carpet, and replace the front door," because that's what they do to every property they buy. (In fact sometimes that's all rehabbers will do to properties they buy.)

You can do the same thing, even if you don't have specialized skills or experience. You just have to be willing to work and manage the project... because you'll use cosmetic problems to your advantage.

Think about it. Nothing turns off potential buyers like cosmetic problems: Peeling paint, rotting deck boards, holes or stains in carpets... and often other people will overlook the fact that underneath the mess is a great deal on a property.

If you're smart, you can use that to your advantage. Buying fixer-uppers to re-sell is a quick way to profit in real estate, especially if you know your market.

You have two basic choices if you decide to get into flipping: You can perform the work yourself or you can hire others to do it for you.

If you perform the work yourself, you can save some money but you also may spend time that you can't afford. If your goal is to only buy one property at a time, fixing it and selling it before buying another, then performing most of the work yourself may be a great idea. If you want to have multiple projects going at the same time... you'll most likely need to hire help.

Hiring other people to do the work for you may cost a little more but it can also save you time and therefore money. Why?

If you're making payments on a loan, the longer you keep the house, the longer you're making payments. By hiring help, you may be able to flip the property more quickly, reducing your total expense.

Remember, time equals money – and the longer you hold the house, especially if your goal is to flip it, the more money it will cost you in taxes, mortgage interest, insurance, and other expenses.

Financial Analysis

There's a simple way to evaluate the investment potential of a fixer-upper. Here's a look at the basic financial calculations involved in buying fixer-upper or rehab properties:

Initial price of property	+
Refurbishing costs	+
Loan expenses	+
Closing costs	=
Total Cost	$_____
New sale price	—
Selling expenses	—

Closing costs	=	
Total Profit	$____	

Let's use a simple example:

Initial price of property	$200,000	+
Refurbishing costs	$20,000	+
Loan expenses	$10,000	+
Closing costs	$5,000	=
Total Cost	$235,000	
New sale price	$290,000	—
Selling expenses	$11,000	—
Closing costs	$5,000	=
Total Profit	**$39,000**	

Many investors, especially novice investors, forget to add expenses for loan payments, closing costs, and selling expenses. Remember: Anything that you spend money on during the process of refurbishing a house is an expense that takes away from your profit.

Choosing Properties

Many people look at a property and say, "Wow, if I can pay $180,000 for this house and put $10,000 in improvements into it, and I sell it for $200,000, I'll make $10,000 really quickly!"

They're wrong. They also need to add in closing cost expenses, interest payments on the mortgage, and the cost of selling the house and closing on that sale, too.

And here's the bottom line: To minimize your risk, you have to buy properties where people actually want to live.

And here's another consideration: Be careful of buying a house near low-income housing. If you buy a house within a mile or two of a low-income section of town, keep an eye on what's happening. One house at a time the low-income section could start to expand… and if it expands close to your home you can have a real problem selling it.

If your house is near a section of town that has bars on the windows or the police have to keep constant patrol, or any of the other signs of a deteriorating neighborhood, the best thing you can do is sell the property as soon as you recognize those signs. You're better off selling the property and getting out from under the mortgage than hanging on waiting for the neighborhood to get better… because it almost never will.

This not only applies when you are buying a property to flip; it also applies to rentals and other income properties. Once a neighborhood starts to deteriorate the other houses in the same area will start to deteriorate as well. If you have a house near a low-income section you will have a harder time renting it.

Let's say your property is in perfect condition: The average rent for the area is $800 per month, and you want to charge $900 per month due to the condition of the house. Your house will more than likely sit vacant because the market will only bring $800 per month.

In that case you'll either have to rent your house at a loss or sell the property.

Choose a Rehab Project That Fits You

Deciding whether a project "fits" you means choosing one you can deal with. In other words, you can handle the work required.

For example, if you can't fix roofs you might not want to rehab a house that needs roof repair. On the other hand, you may be very capable of replacing the roof – or you may just plan to hire a contractor to repair it. Decisions like these depend on your particular comfort zone. Buy a house according to what you are willing to do or not to do… not because your wife's sister's friend knew someone who made a killing by buying and flipping a fixer-upper.

You may have the skills, time, and expertise to do the repair work yourself; if you do and are willing to do it, you can save yourself a lot of money. You might even want to learn how to do repair work.

If you don't know anything about doing the simplest tasks you can buy books on maintenance and repair work, and most home centers now offer classes on how to do everything from building decks to laying ceramic tile. You could also join a Habitat for Humanity project and learn new skills while helping out those less fortunate.

On the other hand, you may not have the time or the desire to do any work at all. In that case you'll need to hire a handyman or a general contractor, or pass up the house and look for one that's in need of minor repair work. You'll have to do some repair work to a fixer-upper – that comes with the territory – but whether you do it yourself or not is up to you.

Refurbishing houses offers another benefit as well – each time you do one, you're improving the quality of your neighborhood or your town. There's a tremendous satisfaction that comes from helping to improve the area you live in.

Basic Renovation and Rehab Guidelines

When you buy a fixer-upper, handyman special, distressed property, or other house you plan to refurbish, rehab, repair, and flip, you'll need to decide how to best proceed. There are some simple guidelines you should follow.

Meet Building Codes

Whatever repairs, upgrades, or improvements you plan do to a house, always be sure they meet the local building code requirements. Any violations or repairs that pop up when you're selling the house can easily give the buyer second thoughts about the property, not to mention a legal reason to back out of the contract.

And, always make repairs and improvements that make a difference based on comparable houses in the neighborhood.

A home buyer who is paying market value expects a house to be in good repair and will hire a home inspector to look for deficiencies. You want to get market value for the property, so make sure you take care of deficiencies. Be smart about it, though.

For example, if you're considering buying a house for $200,000 and one of the improvements needed is a new roof that will cost $18,000, research similar houses first. If you find they sell for $218,000, there's no reason to buy the house. You'll spend way too much money on the roof alone.

Typically, as long as the roof looks OK and passes an inspection, buyers are satisfied. They expect a *good* roof; they won't pay more for a *brand-new* roof. Given the choice among two or more comparable houses, most buyers are unwilling to pay the full premium for a house with a new roof. No doubt the new roof will make the house easier to sell, but few buyers choose to pay the full $18,000 extra.

Don't Plan to Repair the Structure

Costs can easily get out of hand as soon as you start to modify the structure or systems of the house. The easiest fix-ups and the most profitable are those that don't require major structural changes: moving kitchen and bathroom fixtures or opening up load-bearing walls and adding rooms outside the original footprint of the building.

Certainly it's possible to make major structural changes to a property and increase its value far beyond the cost of the upgrade, but consider it only if you are going to live in the property over a period of years so you'll have inflation working for you too.

Kitchens and Bathrooms

Improvements to kitchens and bathrooms will cost and pay back the most. And they're the two key rooms that buyers look at very seriously. Even buyers on a tight budget want the best possible kitchen and bathrooms they can get. Most rehabbers have never bought a house where they didn't do a lot of work in both of these rooms, because they're the most used and most lived-in rooms in the house.

Upgrades in a kitchen can range from a basic cosmetic face-lift of paint, flooring, and appliances to expanding the kitchen into an adjoining room and replacing everything from the ceiling to the floor and all the cabinets and appliances.

Even buyers of a two-bedroom home expect at least a full bath and a half bath to solve the crunch when they're getting ready for work or school in the morning. So by making a one-bath house into a two-bath house by using existing space, you'll recover the investment.

In a bathroom the upgrade can be as basic as scrubbing and wallpapering to gutting it and rebuilding everything with a new bathtub and shower, vanity and countertop, tile, and lighting. In some cases it involves changing the arrangement of fixtures to make a small space work harder.

But don't go crazy with rehabs in those rooms. If you're living in the house while making improvements and the neighborhood supports a luxury bathroom or a gourmet kitchen, you may be able to rationalize their expense. Do the research and find out if comparable properties feature high-end upgrades and what they're selling for before you jump in.

Avoid Extremes – They Rarely Pay Off

Specialized areas like wine cellars, dedicated gyms, tennis courts, and swimming pools seldom give a good return on the investment — that is, unless they are the norm in the neighborhood. Still, the expense is seldom recoverable. Most people won't pay a lot extra for those types of amenities – some may even be willing to pay less, because they have no interest in a tennis court or pool and will be thinking about how much it will cost to get *rid* of them.

Simple Ways to Dramatically Improve the Value of an Investment Property

What do potential buyers notice most about the houses they visit?

That's right: The exterior, the kitchen, and the bathrooms.

The exterior is important because it's the first thing buyers see. A property's curb appeal (or lack of curb appeal) is critical because it's the buyer's first impression.

Imagine you're a potential buyer: You walk up the sidewalk and notice the yard is cluttered, the hedges are overgrown, and the flower beds filled with weeds. You step up to the front door and see peeling paint and cobwebs under the eaves, and you hesitate to reach for the rusty doorknob.

It probably doesn't matter how wonderful the interior of the property may – you're likely to be unimpressed (in fact, you may decide not to even go inside) because your first impression of the property was horrible.

Every experienced real estate broker has stories about potential buyers who saw the exterior of a property and said, "That's okay… we can just drive on and look at another one." Boosting curb appeal is a "must do" improvement to every property you purchase.

The other "must do" items are improvements to kitchens and bathrooms - they're key rooms that buyers look at most closely. Even buyers on a shoestring budget want the best possible kitchen and bathrooms they can get. The average buyer judges the "quality" of a property by the condition of kitchens and bathrooms – they assume if the kitchen looks great the rest of the property is probably great.

Kitchen improvements can range from basic cosmetic makeovers like paint, flooring, and fixtures to expanding the kitchen into an adjoining room and replacing everything from the ceiling to the floor and all the cabinets and appliances. You should focus on basic cosmetic fix-ups, but if the appliances are in poor shape, replacing them may more than pay back the expense. If the kitchen needs a major renovation you may decide not to purchase the property at all, especially if you have limited funds to work with.

In bathrooms, improvements can be as basic as scrubbing and wallpapering to gutting the room and replacing the bathtub and shower, vanity and countertop, tile, and lighting. Again, your goal is to make relatively minor improvements, but replacing an old toilet is an inexpensive improvement you can learn to do yourself. For example, adding shower doors to an existing tub is an inexpensive improvement that greatly enhances the bathroom's appeal.

Bottom line? Fix the house up and make it shine – but don't go overboard. Look at other homes for sale in the same price range, and make sure yours is competitive.

Chapter Twelve

Keep Pushing, Never Give Up On Your Dreams!

Have I eliminated most of your fears? I hope so – investing in real estate isn't complicated. It just takes common sense, a little homework, and a willingness to learn.

The key is to get started. If you already own a home, start looking for another home now. While you're at it, start thinking about what you need to get your current home ready to rent. Start talking to bankers and real estate agents; when you find the right people you can rely on them to help you. And look closely at your current expenses, and find ways to make your money work harder for you. Remember, it's not what you *make*... it's what you keep. It's hard to go to work and ask for a raise... it's easy to give yourself a raise by spending less on items you don't need.

But above all, take the first step. Each step along the way will be easier than the last. Someday you'll look back at what you've accomplished and wonder what you were afraid of.

What were you afraid of? In time you'll realize there was nothing to be afraid of!

If you try, you'll be amazed by how much you learn in a short period of time... and you'll be amazed by the opportunities you'll find to build wealth and go from rags to rental riches!Best of luck—Tim Watro

Chapter Thirteen

What will you do?

We all have the power of thought and we have time. What will you do with both of these. Money will flow through each of us during our lifetime, what will you do with yours? If you want to be poor then spend your money without thought! Spend your money on keeping up with your neighbors and you will be in the vast middle class with lots of monthly bills. Invest in your financial education and learn what an asset is and how to acquire them, you will be choosing to build wealth for you and your family.

So the choice is yours what choice will you make each day with your money? I hope you will choose wealth and by choosing wealth you can make a difference by giving not only money but knowledge to others.

Tim Watro

More Information @ www.HOUSEDOUBLE.com